W9-AUM-530

Giant Book of Dot-to-Dot

A Main Street Book

10 9 8 7 6 5 4

Published by Sterling Publishing Co., Inc.
387 Park Avenue South , New York, N.Y. 10016
Material in this collection was adapted from
Prehistoric Animals © Monica Russo
Dinosaur Dots © Monica Russo
Extinct Animal Dot to Dot   © Monica Russo
Endangered Animal Dot to Dot © Monica Russo
Wildlife Dot to Dot © Monica Russo
Mythical Animals Dot to Dot © Monica Russo
This edition © 1999 by Sterling Publishing Co., Inc.

Manufactured in the United States of America
All rights reserved

Sterling ISBN 0-8069-3681-9

CONTENTS

PREHISTORIC ANIMALS DOT-TO-DOT

Monica Russo

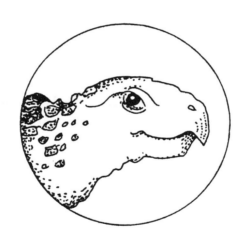

Name:	Archelon
How to say it:	ARR kee lon (*or* arr KEE lon)
Size:	About 12 feet (3.6m) long
When it lived:	During the Cretaceous period, from about 135 million years ago to 70 million years ago.
Where it lived:	Western North America

Archelon was a sea turtle, swimming in an ocean that once covered part of North America.

This big turtle had strong flippers for swimming fast. It ate fish and other ocean animals.

Fossils of other sea turtles have been found in Germany.

Archelon had a sharp
beak-like mouth.

Name:	Baluchitherium
How to say it:	ba luke ih THEER eeum
Size:	About 18 feet (5.4m) tall at the shoulder
When it lived:	About 28 million years ago
Where it lived:	Fossils have been found in Pakistan, India, and Mongolia.

Baluchitherium was probably the largest land mammal that ever lived! It was tall enough to eat the leaves and twigs from trees.

A type of rhinoceros, Baluchitherium had a thick, tough hide, but no horns like today's rhinos. Modern rhinos are only half the size of Baluchitherium.

Another name for Baluchitherium is:

Paraceratherium
(parra seera THEER eeum)

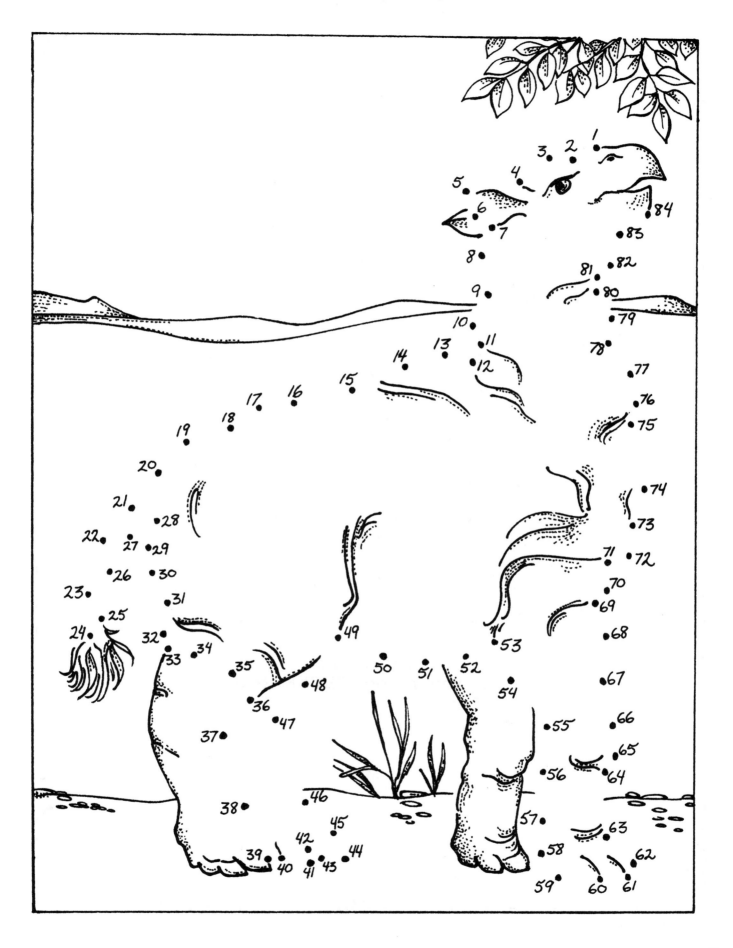

Name:	Basilosaurus
How to say it:	bass illo SAW rus
Size:	About 60 to 70 feet (18–21m) long
When it lived:	About 40 million years ago.
Where it lived:	Fossils have been found in the southeastern U.S.

Basilosaurus was a slim, graceful whale. It was not a type of fish, but a mammal, like modern whales today. Basilosaurus had a small head, but very sharp teeth. It lived on fish and other small ocean animals.

Other prehistoric whales have been found in Africa.

Today's modern Blue Whale is much bigger than Basilosaurus was.

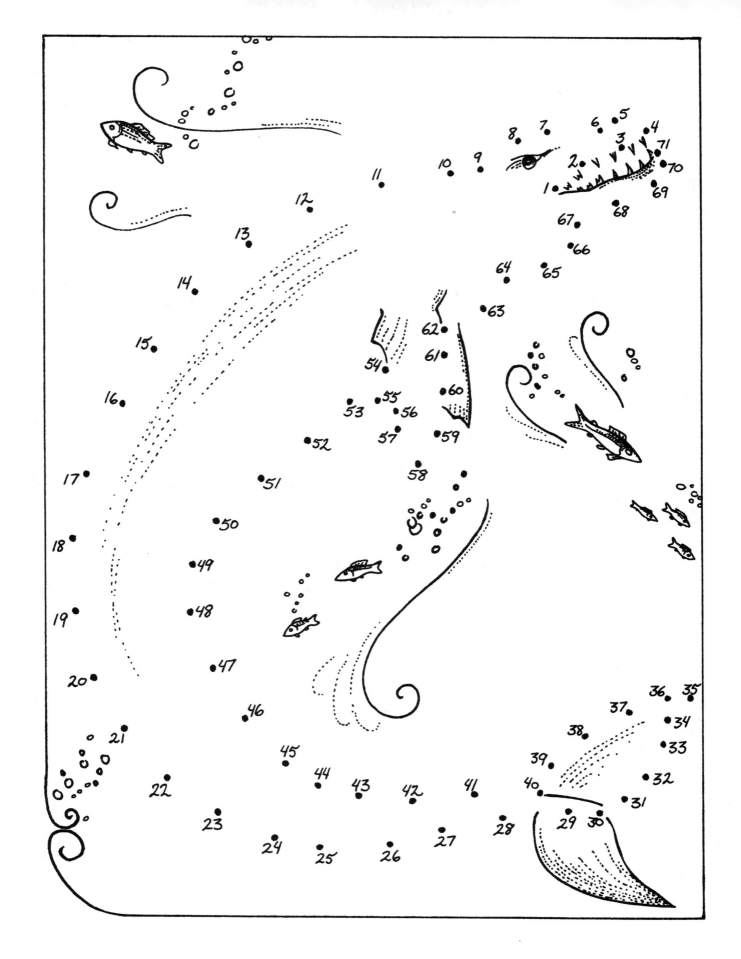

11

Name:	Coelodonta
How to say it:	seelo DON ta
Size:	About six feet (2m) high at the shoulder
When it lived:	During the Pleistocene Ice Age, a period that lasted from about two million years ago to only 20,000 years ago
Where it lived:	Northern Europe and Asia

Coelodonta was a shaggy, woolly Ice Age rhinoceros. It lived in an open, cold, windy habitat called the steppes. There was plenty of thick ice and strong, cold winds. Coelodonta probably roamed the steppes with the huge woolly mammoths called Mammuthus.

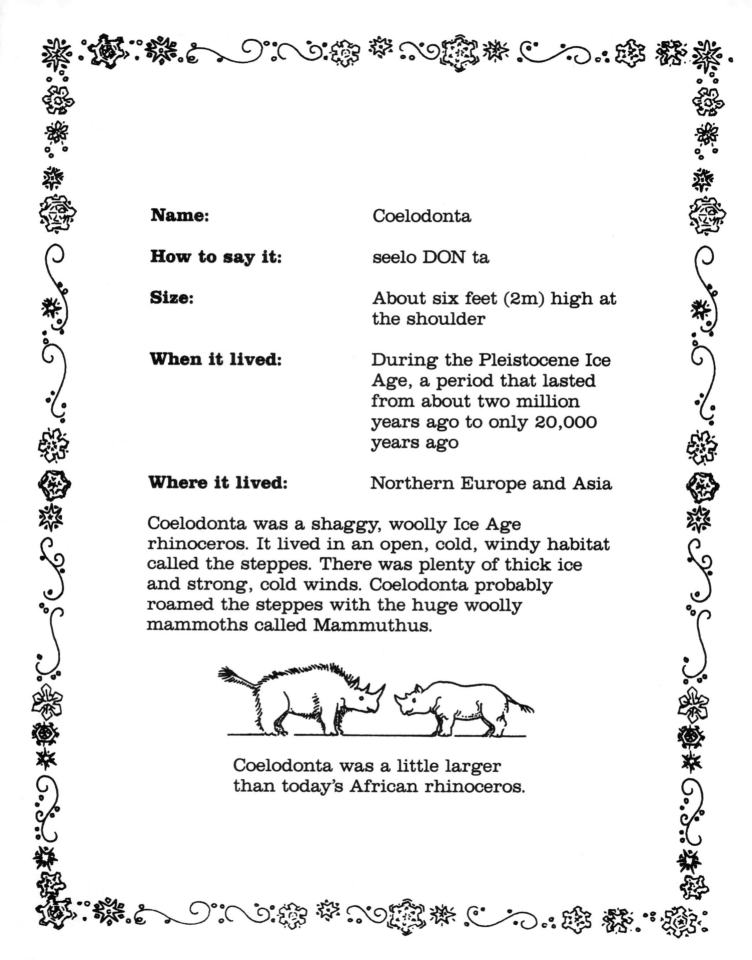

Coelodonta was a little larger than today's African rhinoceros.

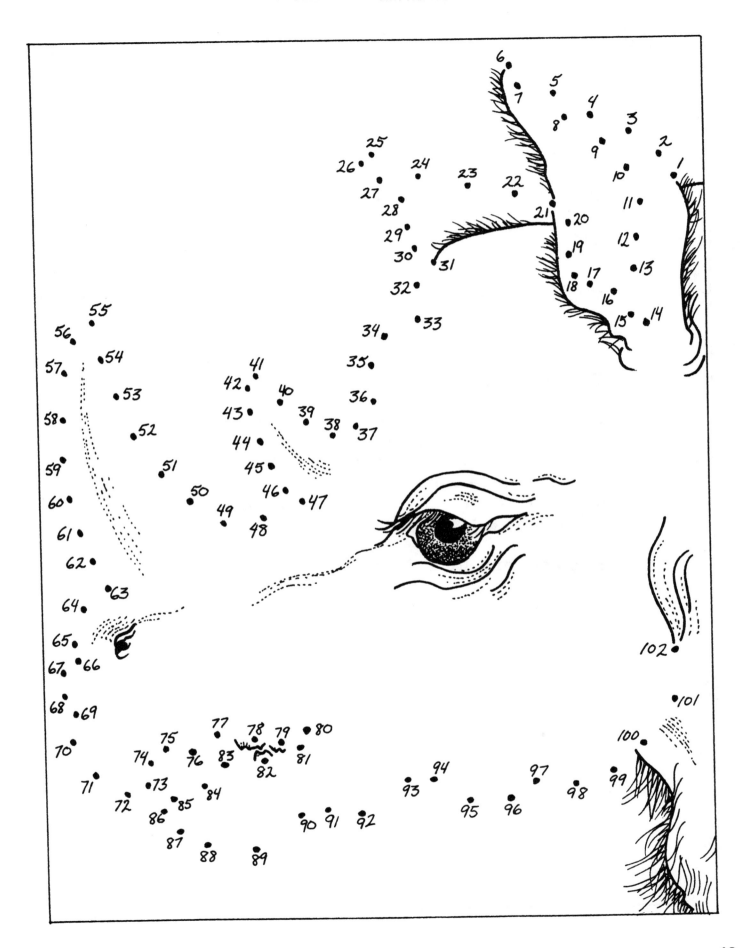

13

Name: Deinosuchus

How to say it: dy-no SU kus

Size: About 40 to 50 feet (12–15m) long

When it lived: During the Cretaceous period, lasting from 135 to 70 million years ago

Where it lived: North America

Deinosuchus lived at the end of the Age of Dinosaurs. It was a huge crocodile, the largest ever known! Some scientists think that Deinosuchus might have been able to catch and eat small dinosaurs, but other scientists think that dinosaurs might have eaten Deinosuchus instead!

Another name for Deinosuchus is:

Phobosuchus
(fobo SU kus)

Name:	Hyracotherium
How to say it:	hy RAK oh THEER eeum
Size:	About two feet (60cm) long—the size of a small dog!
When it lived:	About 50 million years ago, during the Eocene period
Where it lived:	North America and Europe

Hyracotherium is also known as Eohippus (ee oh HIP us) or the Dawn Horse. It was the ancestor of all modern horses. Fossil teeth of Hyracotherium were first found in England by a brickmaker digging in clay in 1838. Fossils of the Dawn Horse were later found in North America, also. Instead of hooves, this animal had four toes in the front, and three toes on its hind feet.

Hyracotherium did not eat grasses like modern horses, but fed on leaves.

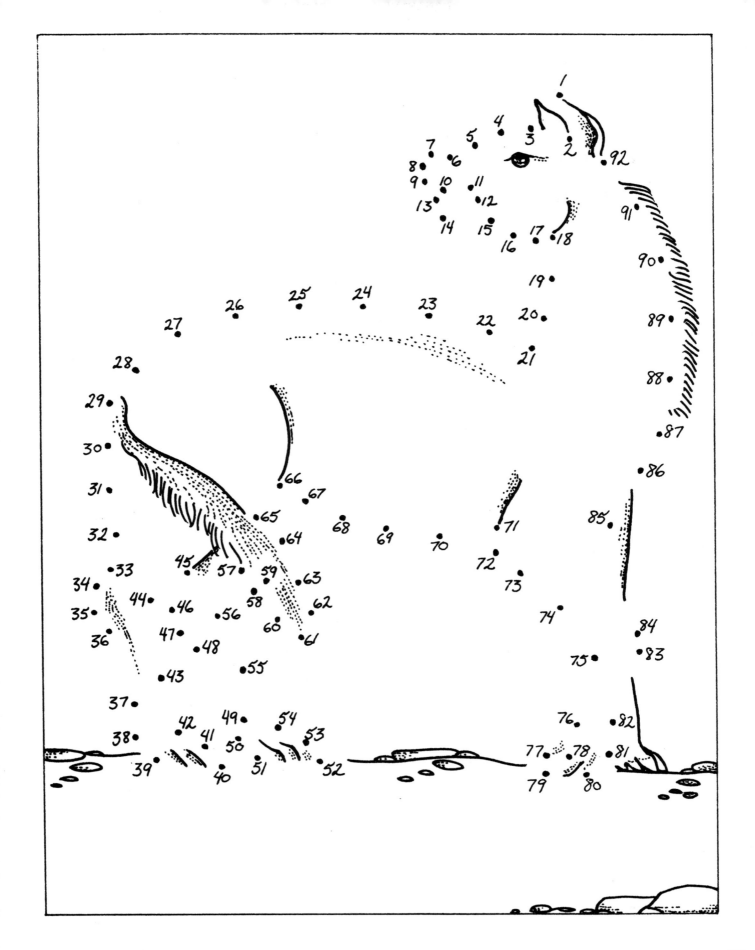

17

Name:	Macrauchenia
How to say it:	may kro CHEE neea
Size:	About 12 feet (3.6m) tall
When it lived:	During the Pleistocene and Pliocene periods: about 10 million years ago to 10,000 years ago
Where it lived:	South America

This unusual animal looked like a combination of a camel and an elephant. Macrauchenia had a long neck and a short trunk. It was probably related to animals with hooves, like horses and deer. It may have fed on leaves and grasses. Several relatives have been found also.

Macrauchenia could have used its
short trunk to pull down leaves
and branches.

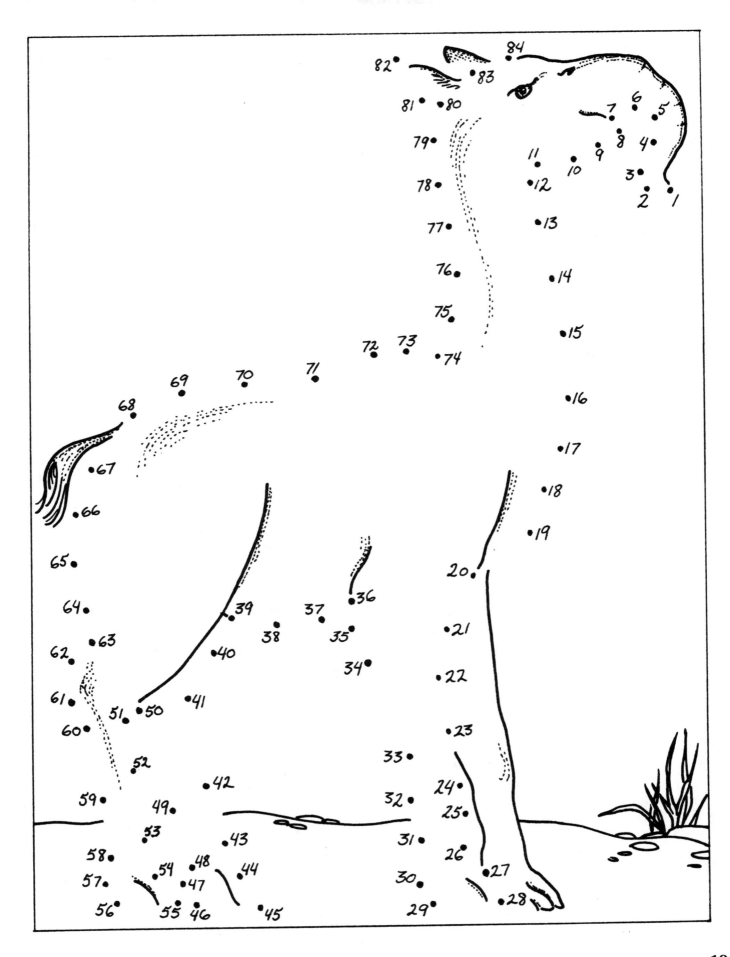

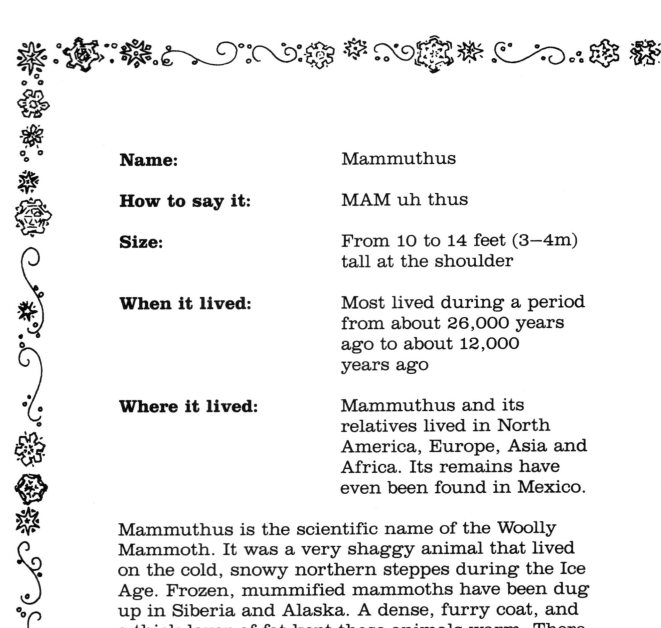

Name:	Mammuthus
How to say it:	MAM uh thus
Size:	From 10 to 14 feet (3–4m) tall at the shoulder
When it lived:	Most lived during a period from about 26,000 years ago to about 12,000 years ago
Where it lived:	Mammuthus and its relatives lived in North America, Europe, Asia and Africa. Its remains have even been found in Mexico.

Mammuthus is the scientific name of the Woolly Mammoth. It was a very shaggy animal that lived on the cold, snowy northern steppes during the Ice Age. Frozen, mummified mammoths have been dug up in Siberia and Alaska. A dense, furry coat, and a thick layer of fat kept these animals warm. There were many different kinds of mammoths, and also different types of mastodons, another relative of modern elephants.

Woolly mammoths were more hairy than elephants are today, and had much longer tusks.

Name:	Mesohippus
How to say it:	MEEZ oh HIP us
Size:	About two feet (60cm) tall at the shoulder
When it lived:	During the Oligocene period, which lasted from about 40 million years ago to 25 million years ago
Where it lived:	Western North America

Mesohippus was an early type of horse. It lived after Hyracotherium (the Dawn Horse on page 38), and looked more like a horse. It had three toes on each foot. Mesohippus was about the size of a sheep or goat. Since grasslands were beginning to spread across North America at the time it lived, this animal was able to eat grasses along with the leaves of shrubs.

Did Mesohippus have spots or stripes—or was it a solid color? No one really knows for sure.

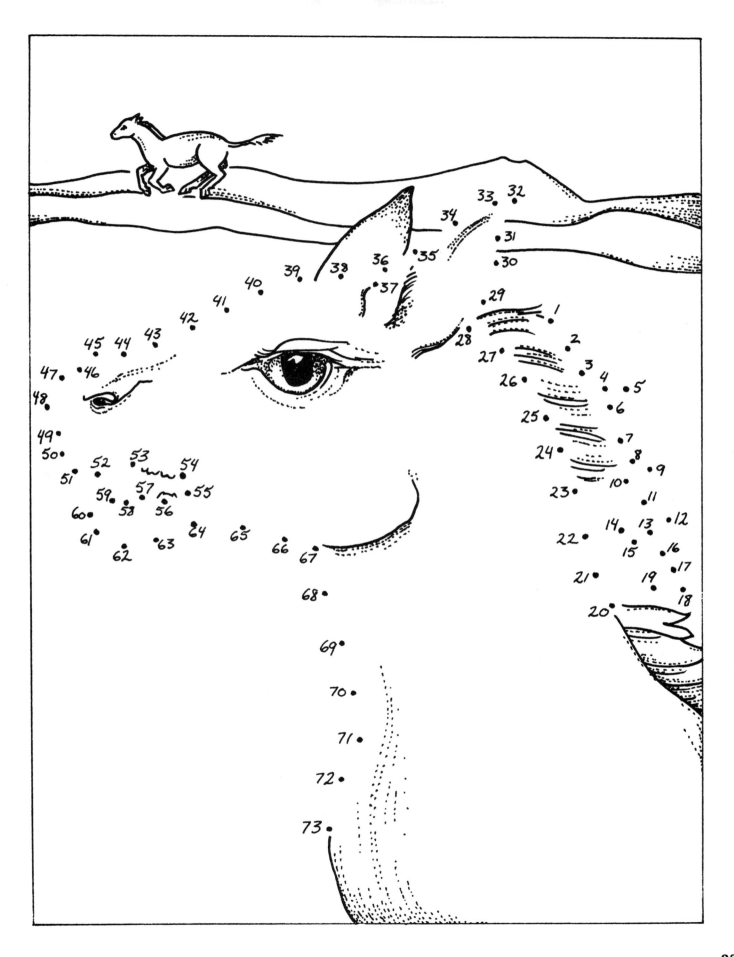

Name:	Moeritherium
How to say it:	MOR ih THEER eeum
Size:	About two to three feet (60cm–1m) at the shoulder
When it lived:	About 20 to 40 million years ago
Where it lived:	North Africa and Egypt

Moeritherium was one of the earliest ancestors of the modern elephant. It had short thick legs and a heavy body. Much smaller than an elephant, Moeritherium was only the size of a sheep.

It probably had a tough hide like an elephant or rhino today.

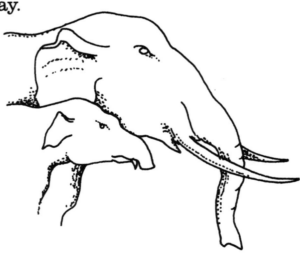

Moeritherium had a very short
trunk and small tusks, compared
to a modern elephant.

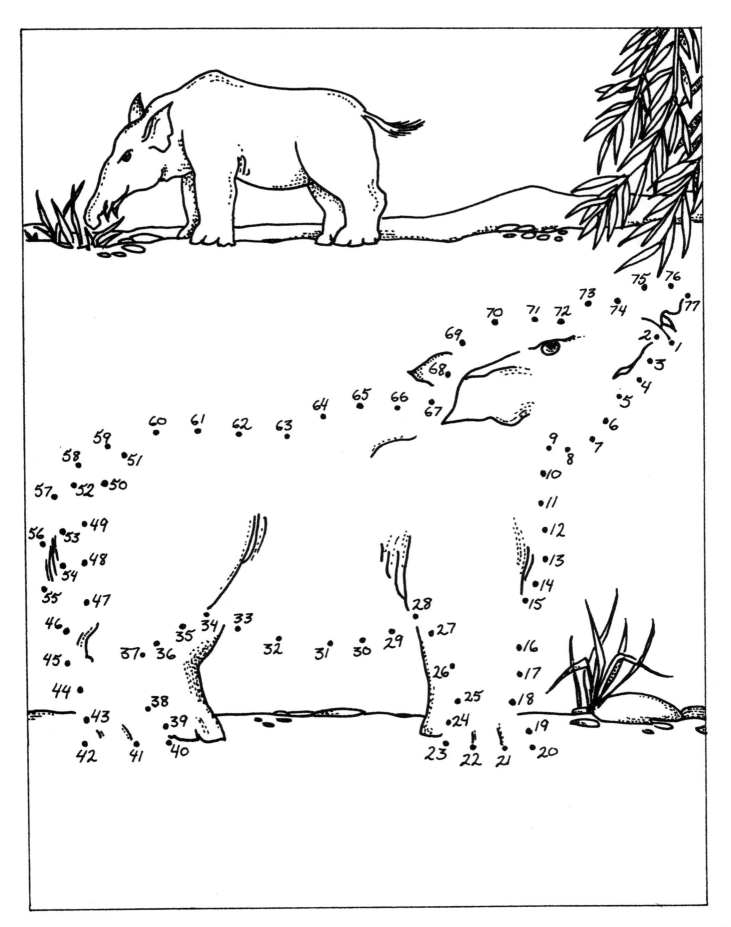

Name:	Moropus
How to say it:	moor OH pus
Size:	Its head was about seven feet (2m) from the ground
When it lived:	During the Miocene period, which lasted from about 25 to 10 million years ago
Where it lived:	Western North America

The forelegs of Moropus were longer than its hind legs, so the back of this mammal sloped downward. It was about as big as a large horse is today.

Moropus was a vegetarian, eating leaves and probably digging up roots with its strong claws.

Moropus may have been able to
stand up on its hind legs to eat
tree leaves.

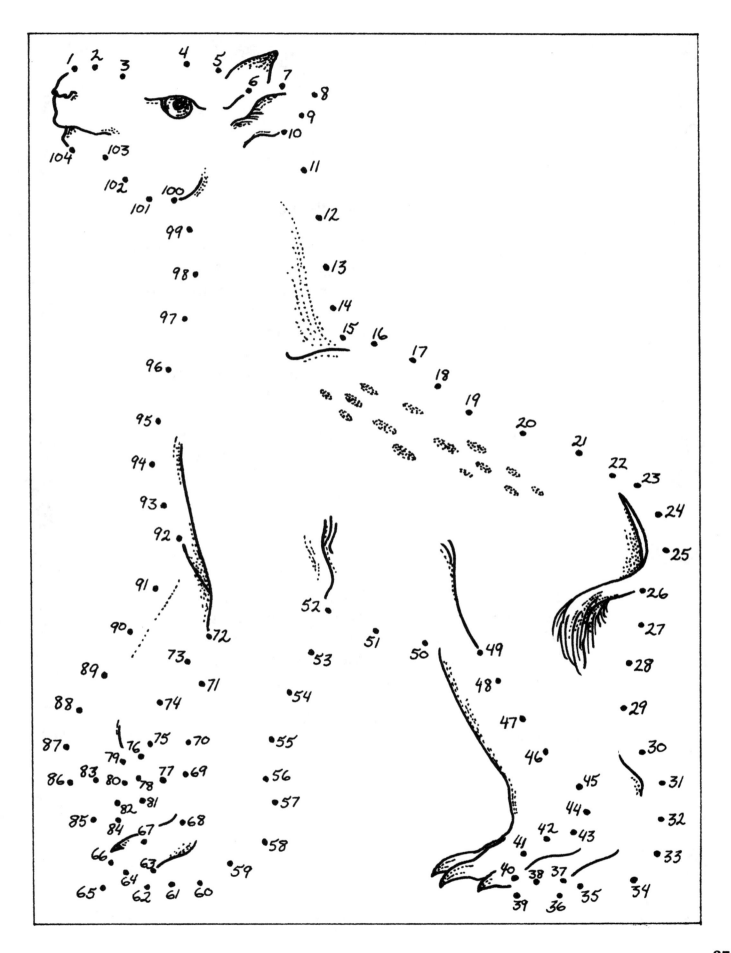

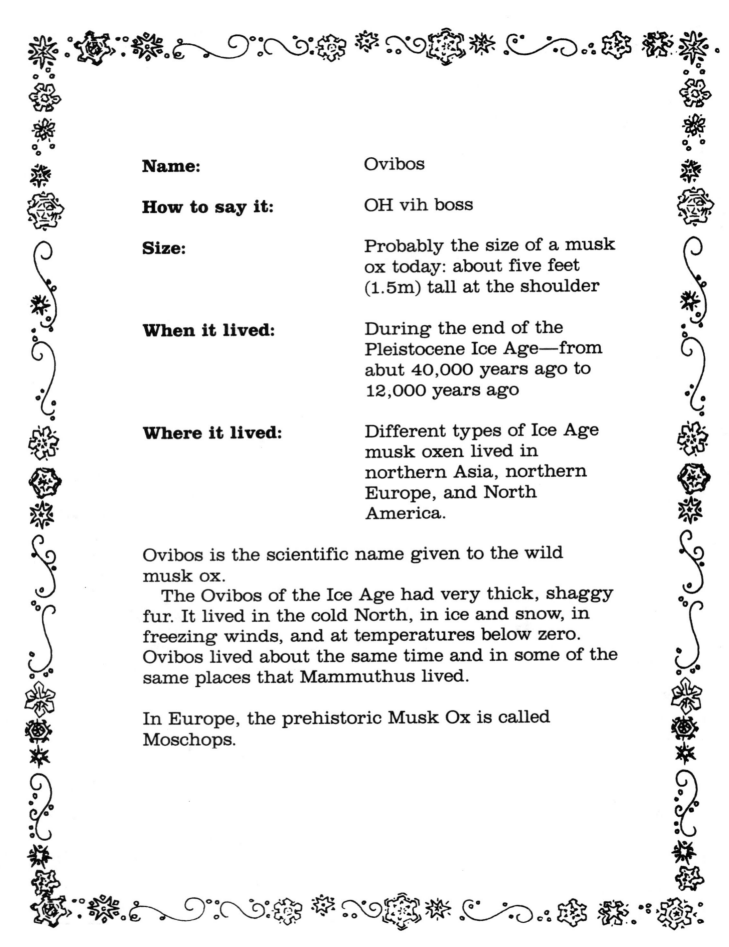

Name:	Ovibos
How to say it:	OH vih boss
Size:	Probably the size of a musk ox today: about five feet (1.5m) tall at the shoulder
When it lived:	During the end of the Pleistocene Ice Age—from abut 40,000 years ago to 12,000 years ago
Where it lived:	Different types of Ice Age musk oxen lived in northern Asia, northern Europe, and North America.

Ovibos is the scientific name given to the wild musk ox.

The Ovibos of the Ice Age had very thick, shaggy fur. It lived in the cold North, in ice and snow, in freezing winds, and at temperatures below zero. Ovibos lived about the same time and in some of the same places that Mammuthus lived.

In Europe, the prehistoric Musk Ox is called Moschops.

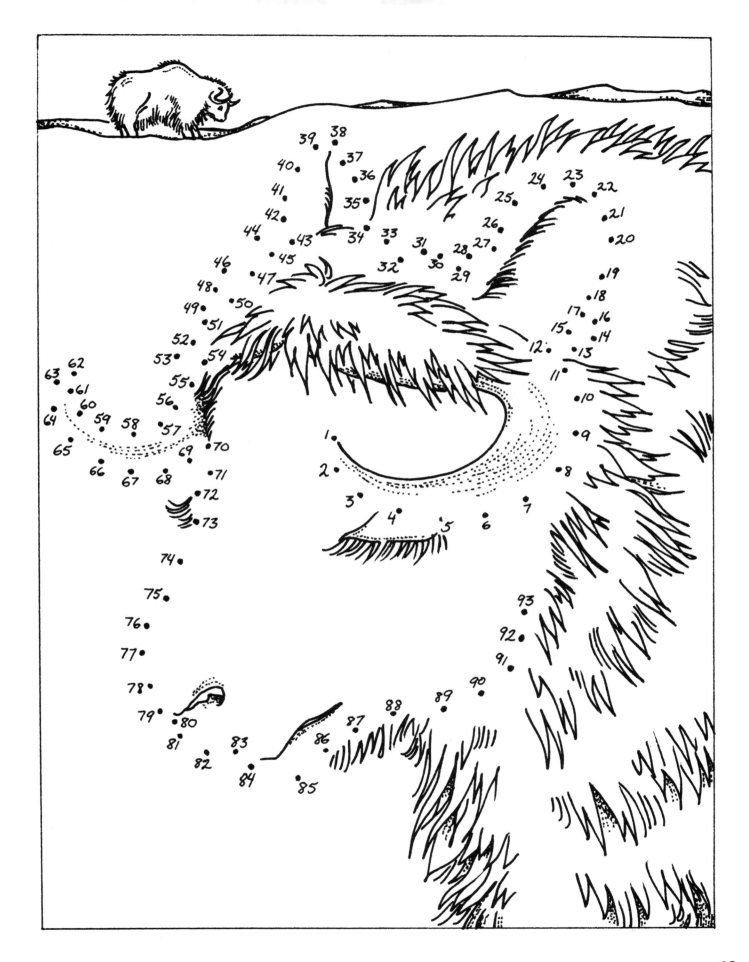

Name:	Paramys
How to say it:	pare AM eez
Size:	About two feet (60cm) long, including its tail
When it lived:	During the Eocene period, which lasted from about 60 to 40 million years ago
Where it lived:	Western North America

Paramys was probably much like a squirrel, scampering through tree branches and climbing straight up the trunks of trees. A rodent, Paramys had strong teeth that it used to gnaw open hard seeds and nuts. Paramys was probably as comfortable running on the ground as it was climbing around high in the trees. It probably ate seeds, berries, nuts and roots.

Name:	Phorusrhacos
How to say it:	FOR us RAK ose
Size:	Five to six feet (1.5—2m) tall
When it lived:	About 20 to 30 million years ago
Where it lived:	South America

Phorusrhacos had feathers, but it couldn't fly—its wings were much too small.

This prehistoric bird had a large head with a strong, curved beak. It was a meat-eater, that ran after small animals on its strong legs.

There were no dinosaurs left when Phorusrhacos lived. Scientists think that this big bird may be an ancestor of today's graceful, long-legged crane.

Name:	Protoceratid
How to say it:	PRO to SARE ah tid
Size:	About three to four feet (.9—1.2m) at the shoulder
When it lived:	During the Miocene and Pliocene periods, from about 25 million years ago to two million years ago
Where it lived:	Western North America

Protoceratid is a name for a whole group of prehistoric animals. They had hooves, and probably looked like today's deer and antelopes.

Some Protoceratids had unusual horns. The Protoceratid shown here had four horns, with two of them towards the end of its nose! These animals may have grazed in herds or small groups.

Protoceratid is a combination of ancient Greek words:

Proto means "first"
ceratid means "horned"

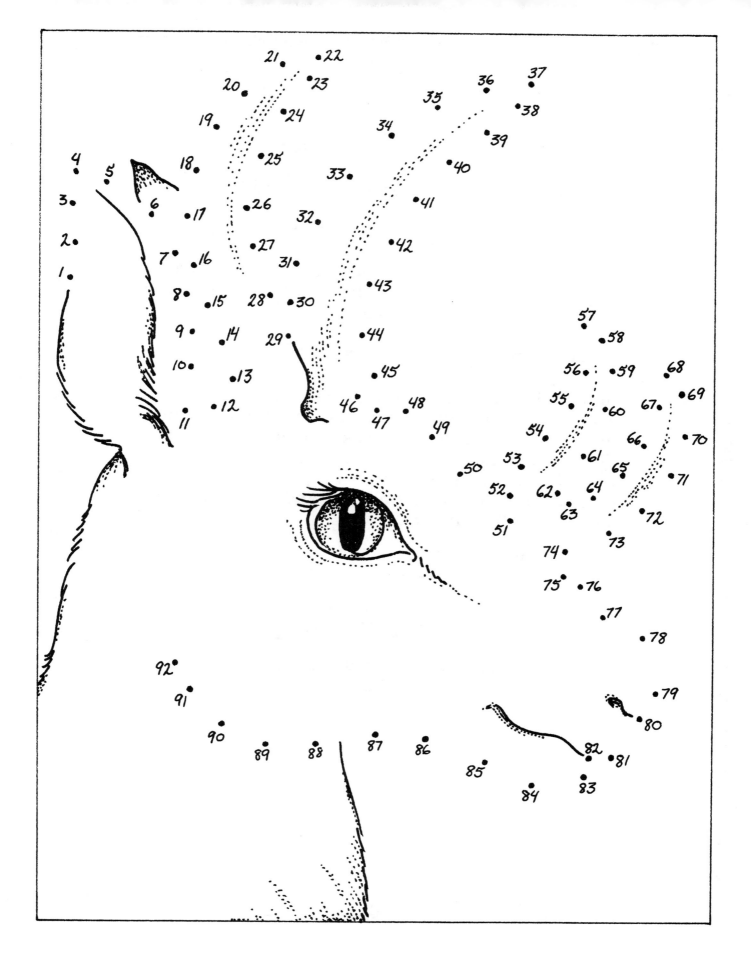

Name:	Ramapithecus
How to say it:	ramma PITH ah kus
Size:	About five feet (1.5m) tall
When it lived:	About 14 million years ago, to about eight million years ago
Where it lived:	Africa and Asia

Ramapithecus is one of the earliest known ancestors of humans. It probably spent a lot of time in trees, but it could also walk upright a little bit. This animal had long arms and was covered with short fur. Ramapithecus was a type of prehistoric ape, and all apes and monkeys—and humans—have hands with five fingers.

Ramapithecus lived long after
the last dinosaur.

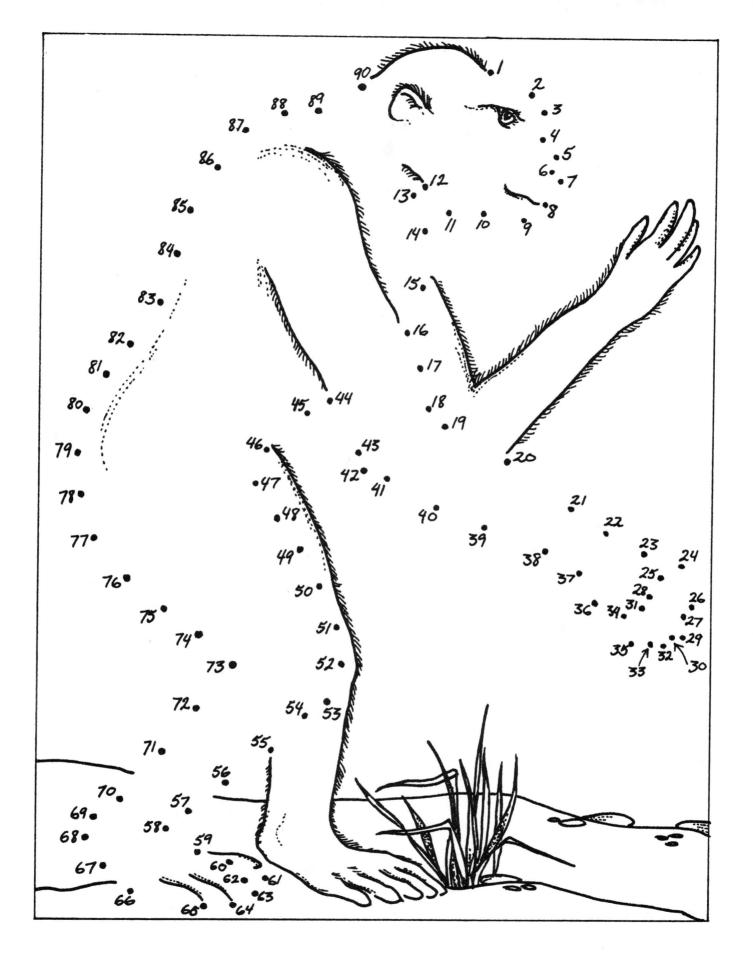

Name:	Smilodon
How to say it:	SMY lo don
Size:	About 10 feet (3m) long, from nose to tip of tail
When it lived:	During the Pleistocene period, lasting from about two million years ago to about 10,000 years ago
Where it lived:	North America, with relatives in South America and Europe

Smilodon was a big, meat-eating cat that lived during the Ice Age. It hunted and ate other prehistoric animals. Smilodon had long, large fangs. Many skeletons of this huge cat have been found at the La Brea tar pits near Los Angeles, California.

Other names for Smilodon are:

Saber-toothed tiger
Stabbing cat

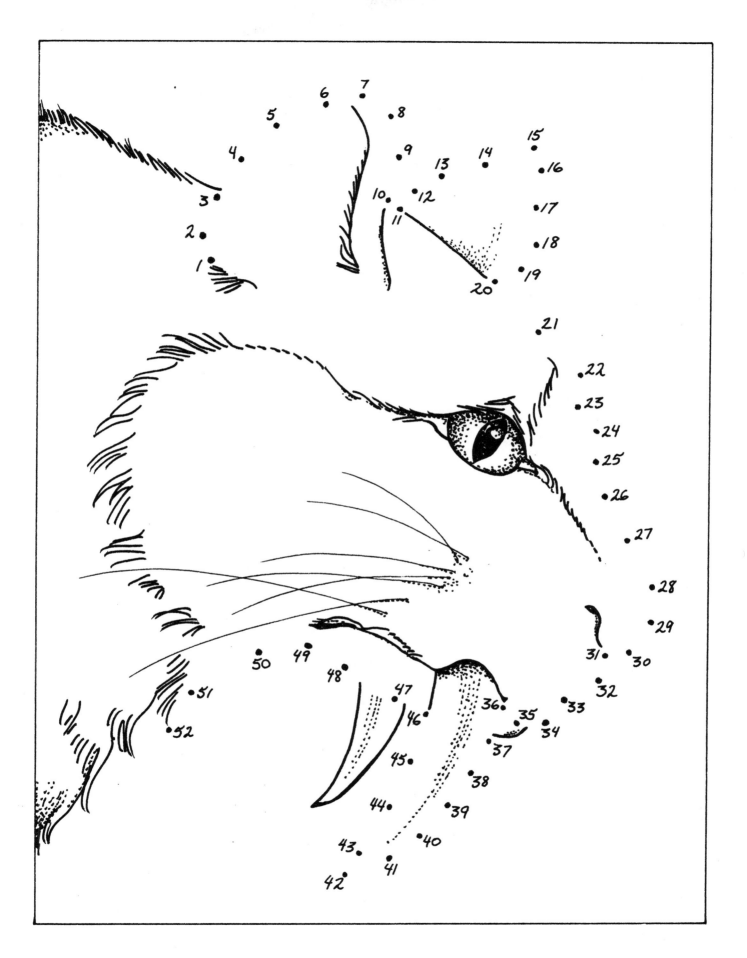

DINOSAUR DOTS

Monica Russo

Name:	Albertosaurus
How to say it:	al BER toe SAW ris
Size:	About 28 feet (8.4m) long It weighed about two tons (1.8 tonnes).
What it ate:	Meat
When it lived:	65 to 75 million years ago
Fossils have been found in:	Alberta, Canada

Albertosaurus

Albertosaurus probably looked like a small Tyrannosaurus (see page 94).

It used to be called Gorgosaurus (GOR go SAW ris).

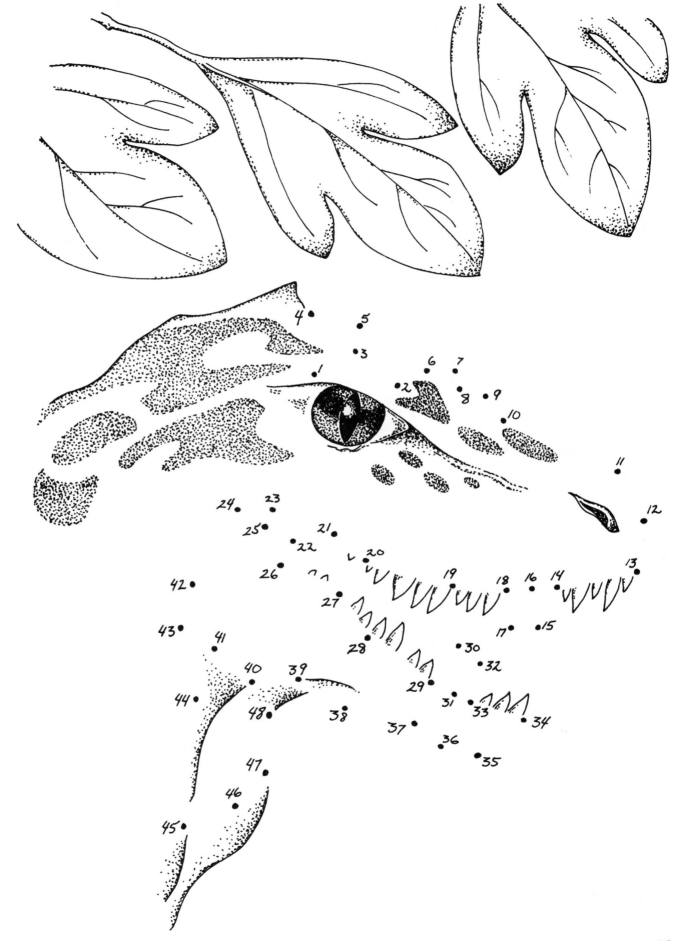

Name:	Apatosaurus
How to say it:	ah PAT oh SAW ris
Size:	About 50 to 80 feet (15–24m) long It weighed around 30 tons (27 tonnes).
What it ate:	Plants
When it lived:	140 million years ago
Fossils have been found in:	Wyoming and Colorado, U.S.A.

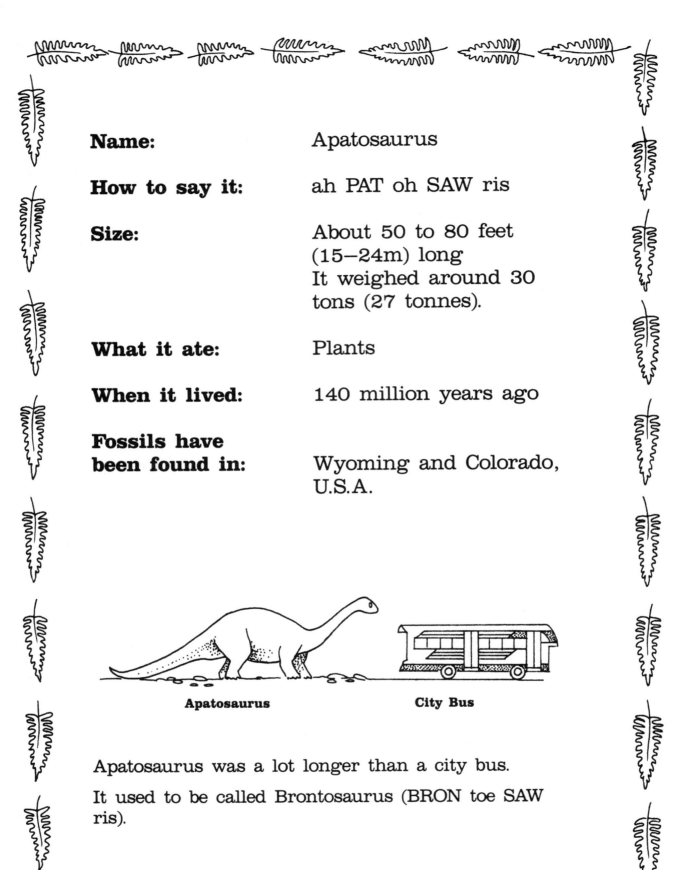

Apatosaurus   **City Bus**

Apatosaurus was a lot longer than a city bus.

It used to be called Brontosaurus (BRON toe SAW ris).

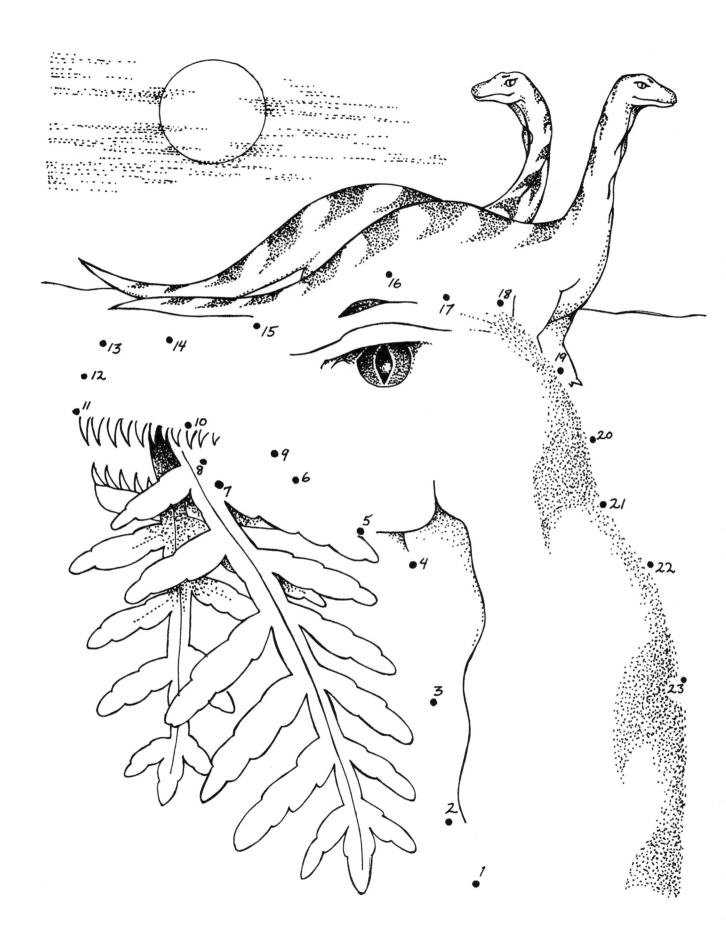

Name: Corythosaurus

How to say it: ko RITH ah SAW ris

Size: About 33 feet (9.9m) long

What it ate: Tough plants, like pine needles and twigs

When it lived: About 75 to 95 million years ago

Fossils have been found in: Alberta, Canada

There were more kinds of plant-eating dinosaurs than meat-eaters. The meat-eaters just get more attention!

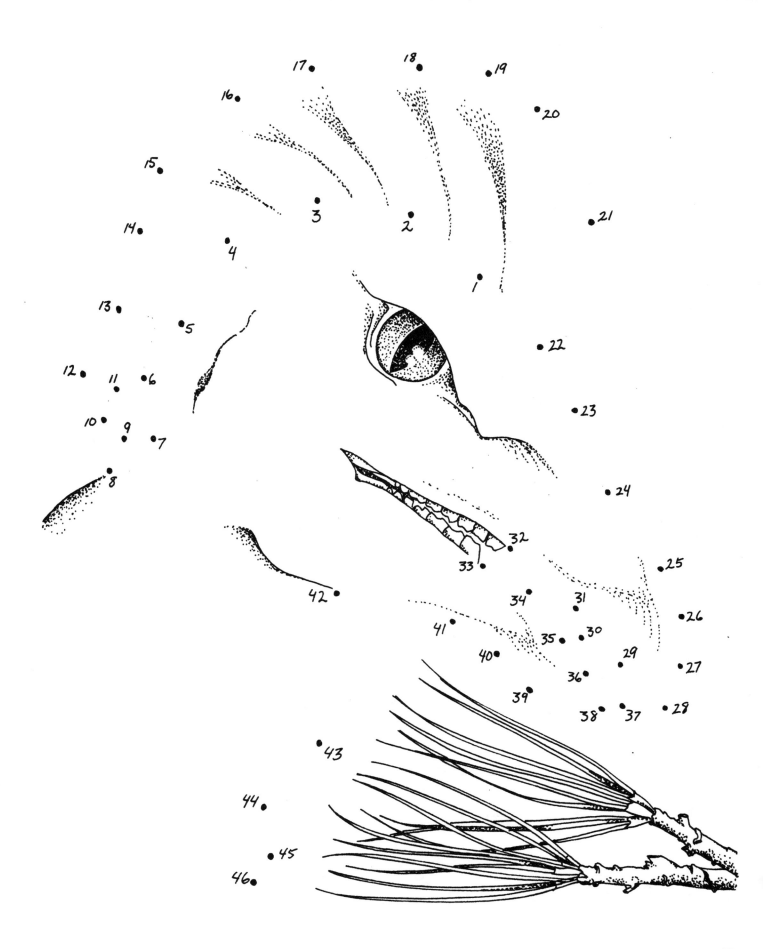

Name:	Deinonychus
How to say it:	DY no NIK us or dine ON ik us
Size:	About 10 to 13 feet (3–3.9m) long It was five feet (1.5m) tall.
What it ate:	Meat
When it lived:	70 to 100 million years ago
Fossils have been found in:	Montana, U.S.A.

Some scientists think this dinosaur may have had some feathers.

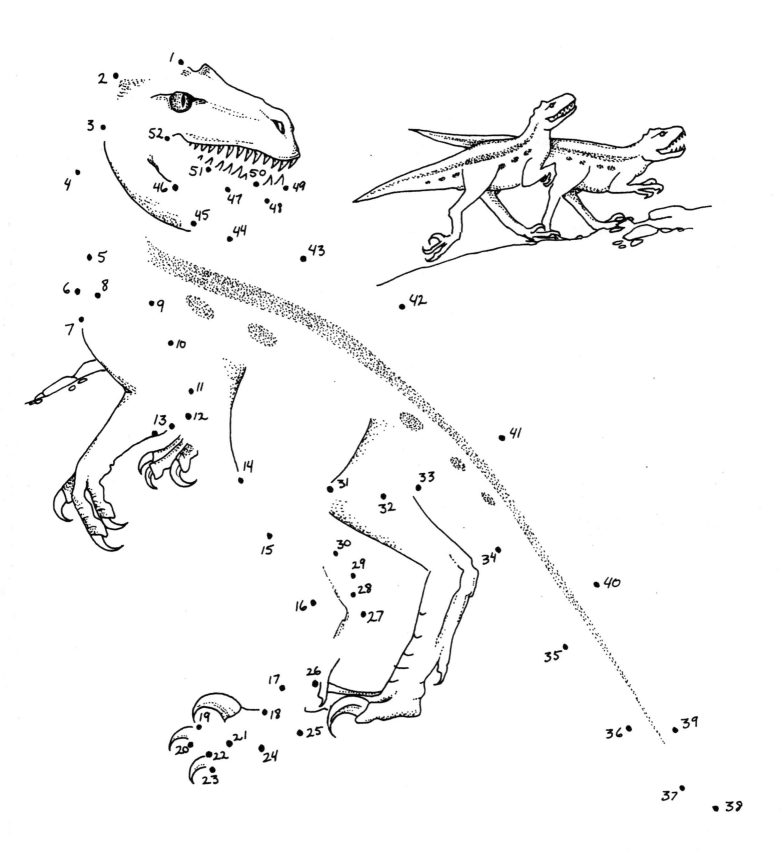

Name:	Dilophosaurus
How to say it:	dy LO fah SAW ris
Size:	About 20 feet (6m) long
What it ate:	Meat
When it lived:	About 180 to 190 million years ago
Fossils have been found in:	Arizona, U.S.A.

Dilophosaurus had weak jaws and probably hunted only for small animals.

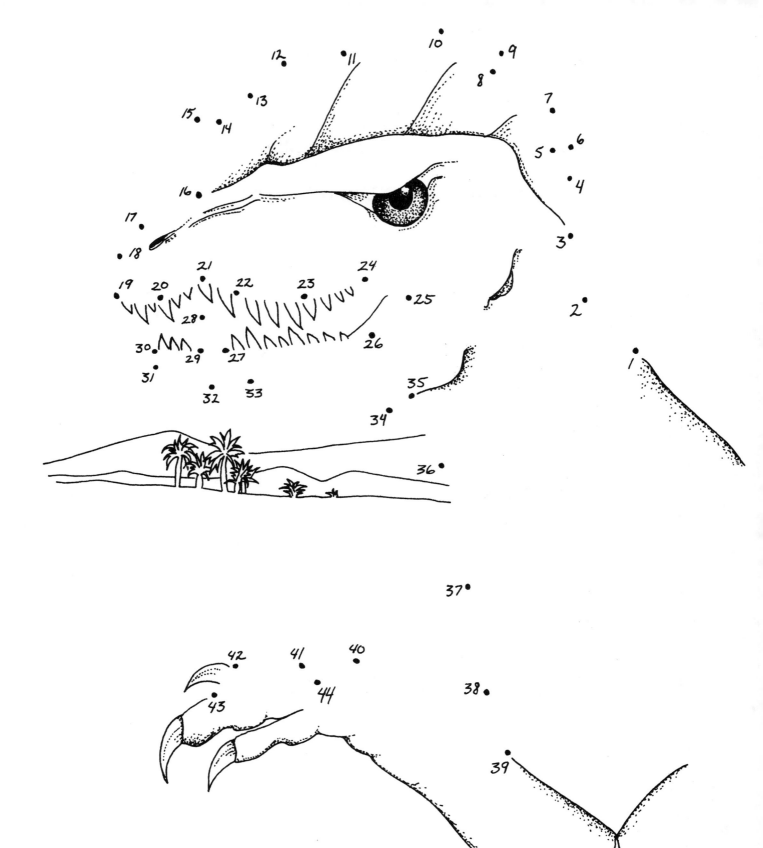

51

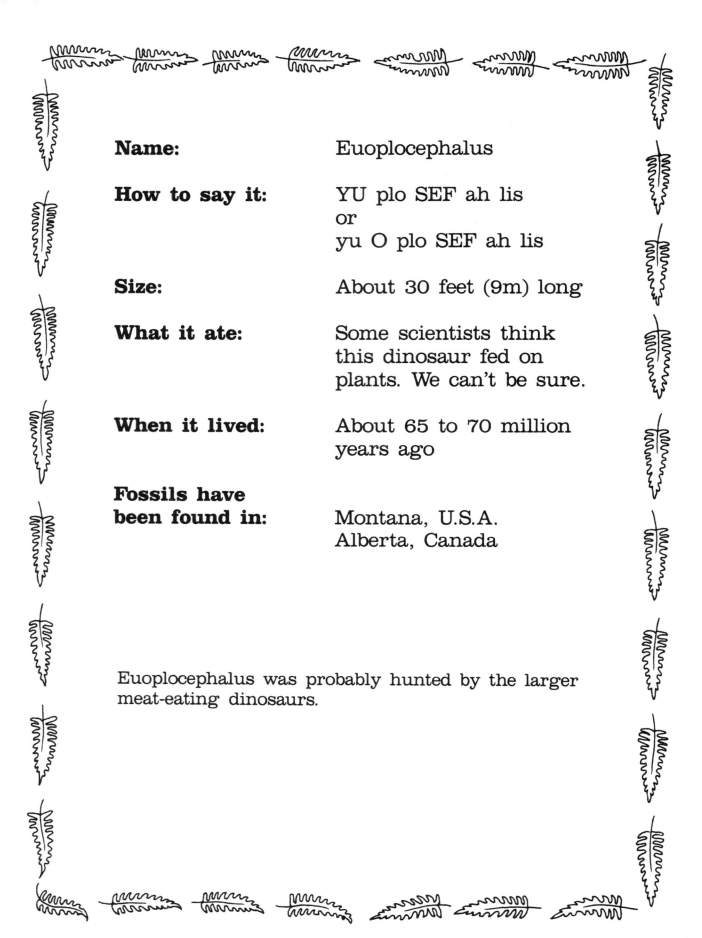

Name:	Euoplocephalus
How to say it:	YU plo SEF ah lis or yu O plo SEF ah lis
Size:	About 30 feet (9m) long
What it ate:	Some scientists think this dinosaur fed on plants. We can't be sure.
When it lived:	About 65 to 70 million years ago
Fossils have been found in:	Montana, U.S.A. Alberta, Canada

Euoplocephalus was probably hunted by the larger meat-eating dinosaurs.

Name:	Gallimimus
How to say it:	GAL ah MY mis
Size:	About 13 feet (3.9m) long
What it ate:	Some scientists think Gallimimus ate the eggs of other dinosaurs.
When it lived:	About 65 to 70 million years ago
Fossils have been found in:	Mongolia

Gallimimus had no teeth. It could have eaten eggs, and maybe insects, too.

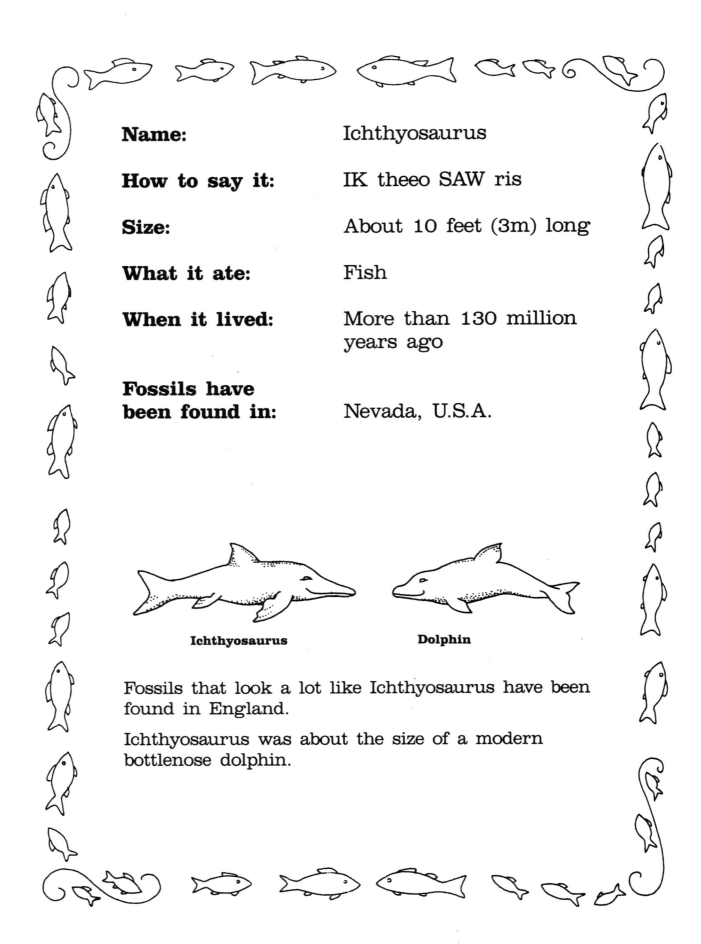

Name:	Ichthyosaurus
How to say it:	IK theeo SAW ris
Size:	About 10 feet (3m) long
What it ate:	Fish
When it lived:	More than 130 million years ago
Fossils have been found in:	Nevada, U.S.A.

Ichthyosaurus   **Dolphin**

Fossils that look a lot like Ichthyosaurus have been found in England.

Ichthyosaurus was about the size of a modern bottlenose dolphin.

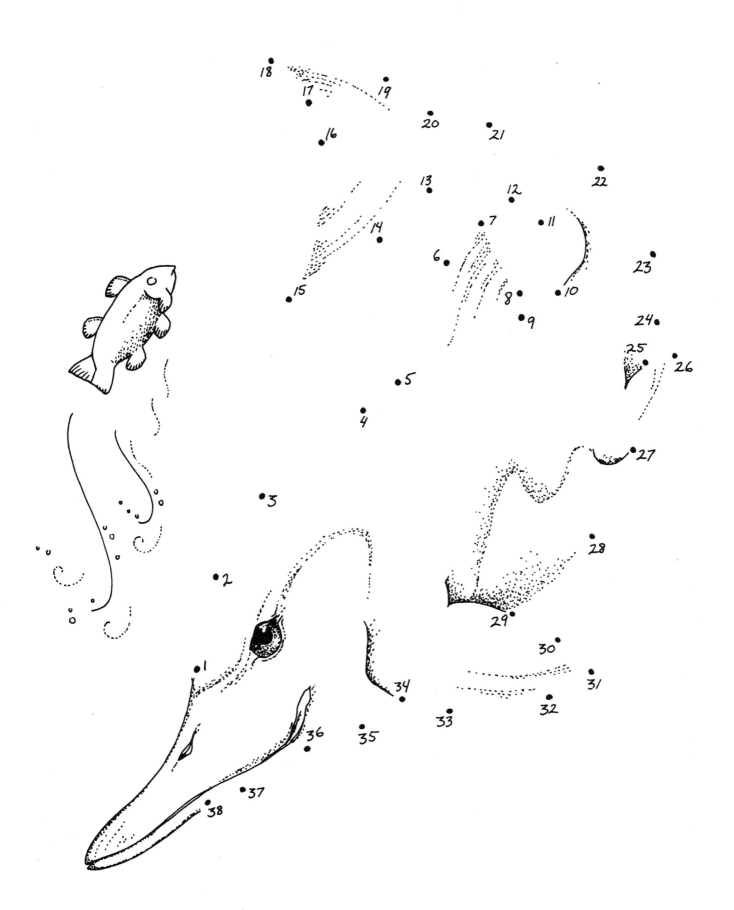

Name:	Monoclonius
How to say it:	monno KLO nee is
Size:	Up to 18 feet (5.4m) long
What it ate:	Plants
When it lived:	About 75 to 80 million years ago
Fossils have been found in:	Montana, U.S.A. Alberta, Canada

Another name for this dinosaur is Centrosaurus (sen tro SAW ris).

Name:	Oviraptor
How to say it:	OH vih RAP tor
Size:	About 6 to 9 feet (1.8–2.7m) long
What it ate:	Eggs and perhaps some plants
When it lived:	About 70 to 80 million years ago
Fossils have been found in:	The Gobi Desert, Mongolia

Dinosaur names are tricky to say or spell because they come from ancient Greek or Latin words. Sometimes, even scientists don't agree on how to say a name!

Oviraptor means "egg robber" in Latin.

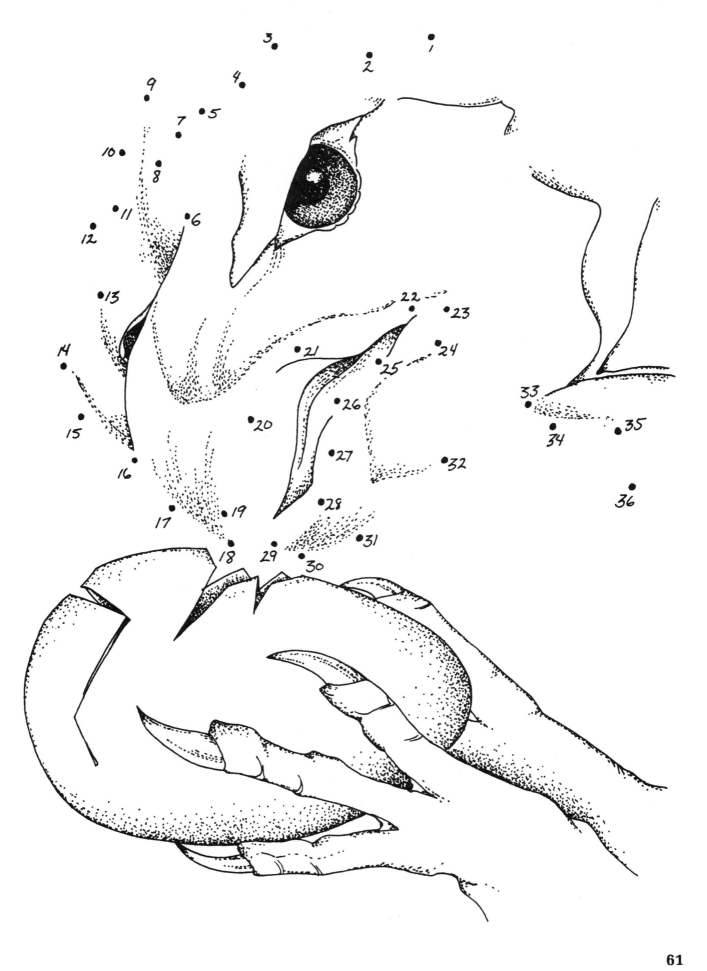

61

Name:	Psittacosaurus
How to say it:	SIT ah ko SAW ris
Size:	Nearly seven feet (2.1m) long
What it ate:	Plants
When it lived:	About 95 million years ago
Fossils have been found in:	Mongolia

Fossils of bones do not give any clues to the colors of dinosaurs. Some dinosaurs may have been plain grey like elephants, and others brightly colored like parrots.

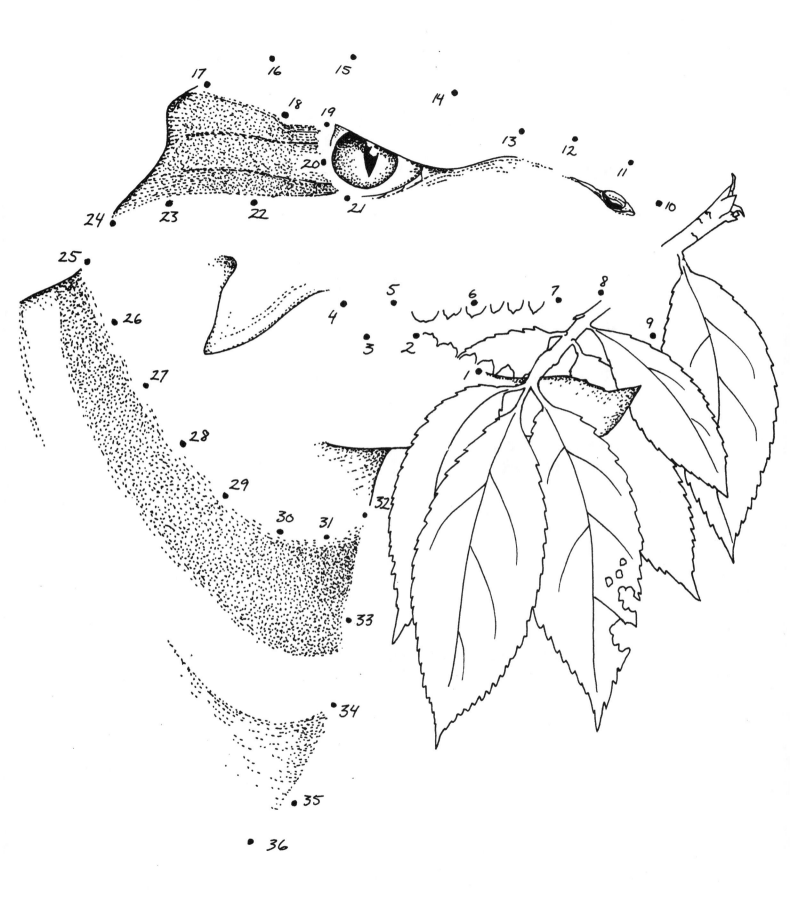

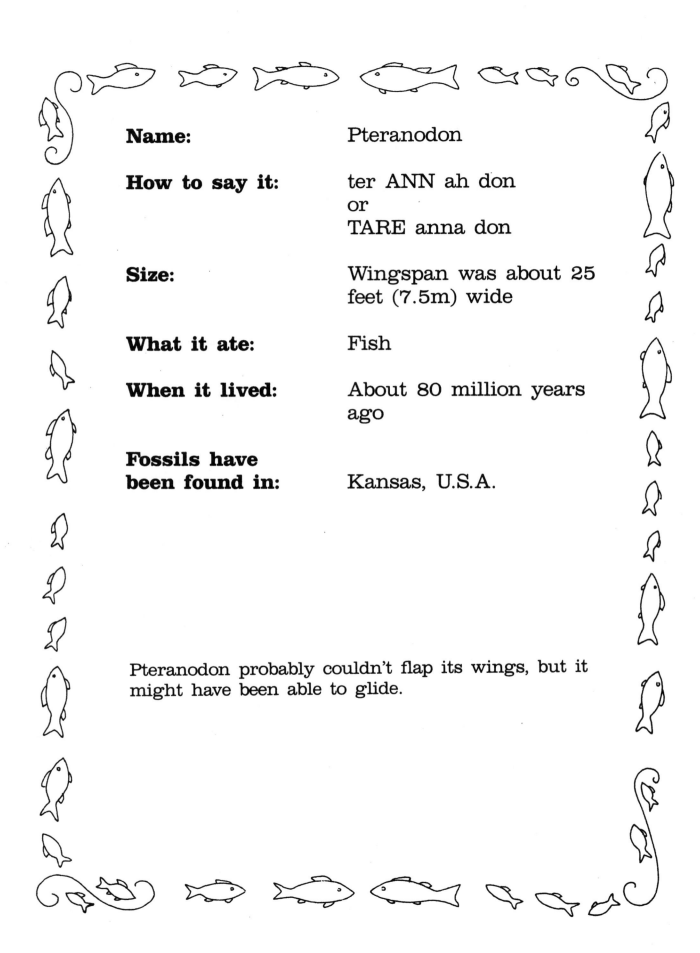

Name:	Pteranodon
How to say it:	ter ANN ah don or TARE anna don
Size:	Wingspan was about 25 feet (7.5m) wide
What it ate:	Fish
When it lived:	About 80 million years ago
Fossils have been found in:	Kansas, U.S.A.

Pteranodon probably couldn't flap its wings, but it might have been able to glide.

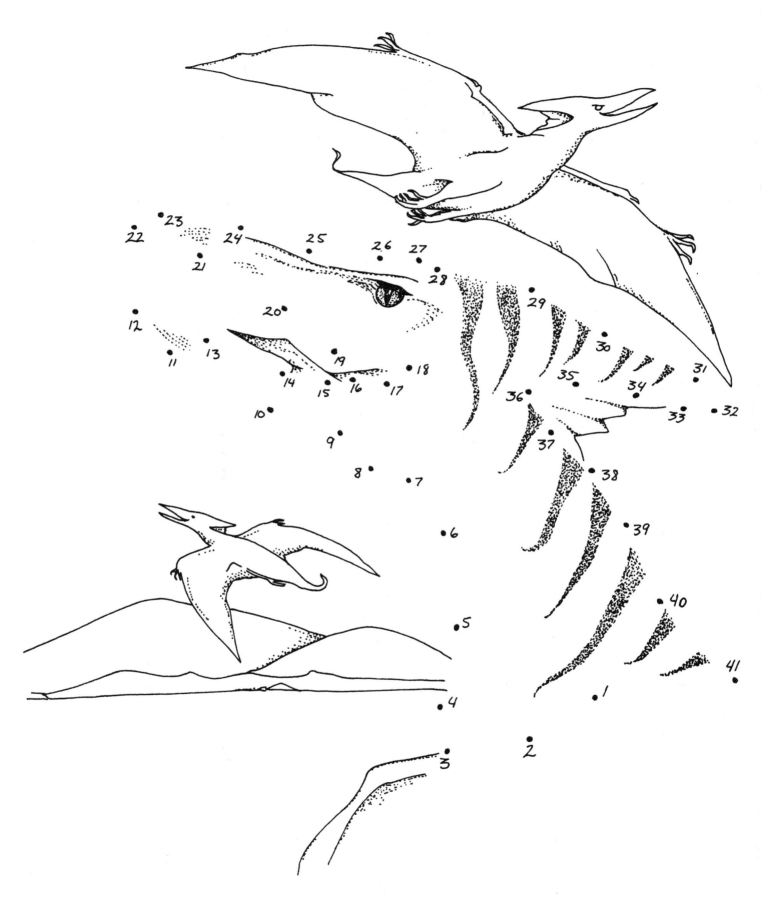

Name:	Pterodactylus
How to say it:	terra DAK till us
Size:	Wingspan of about 18 inches (45 cm) across
What it ate:	Insects, fish, worms
When it lived:	About 150 million years ago
Fossils have been found in:	Bavaria, Germany

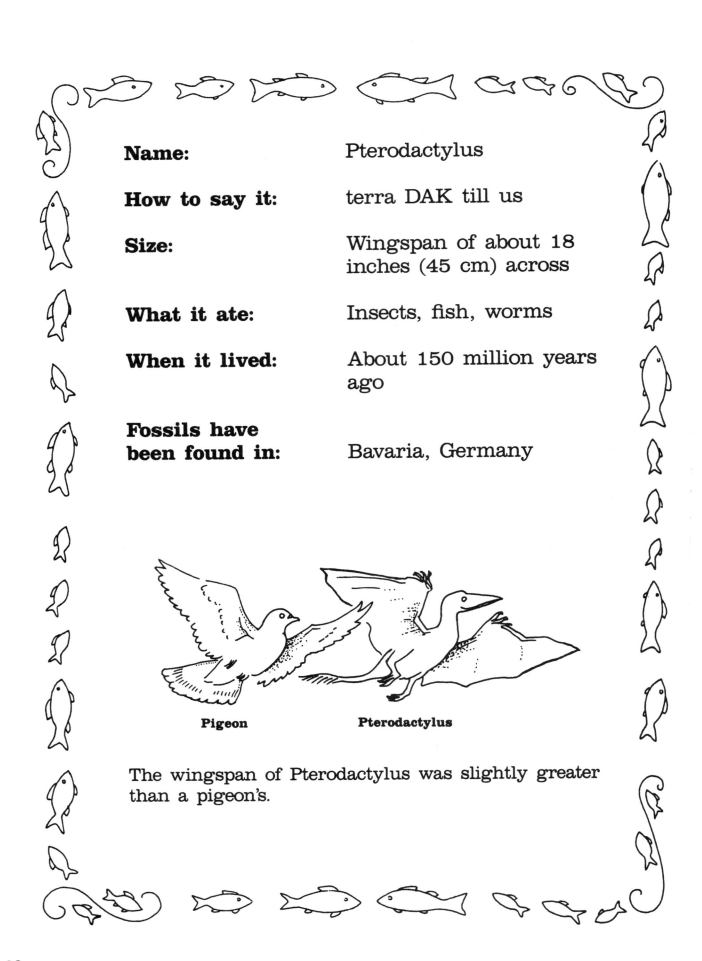

Pigeon   Pterodactylus

The wingspan of Pterodactylus was slightly greater than a pigeon's.

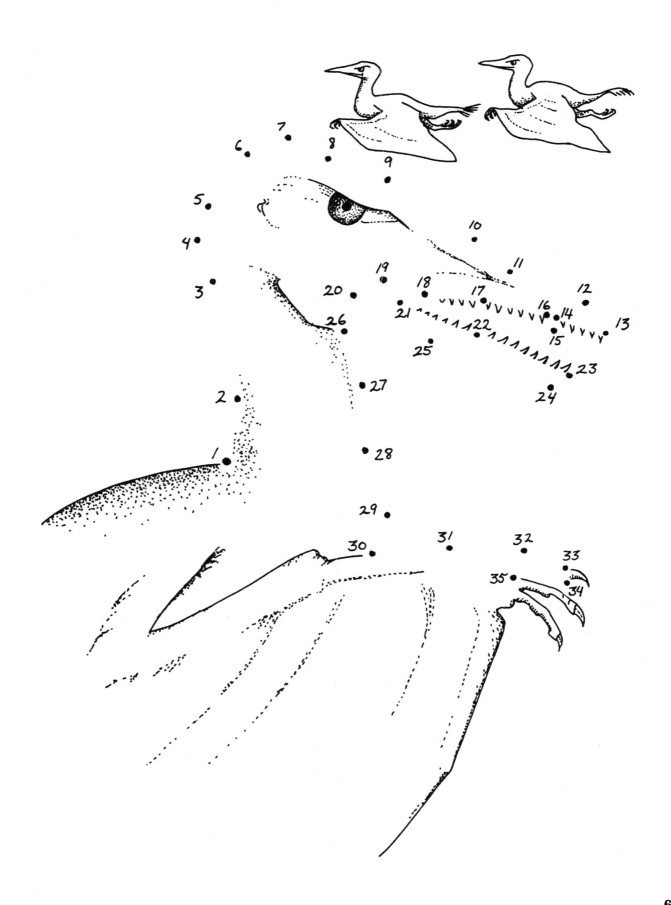

67

Name:	Silvisaurus
How to say it:	SILL vah SAW ris
Size:	Up to 12 feet (3.6m) long
What it ate:	Probably plants
When it lived:	About 95 to 100 million years ago
Fossils have been found in:	Kansas, U.S.A.

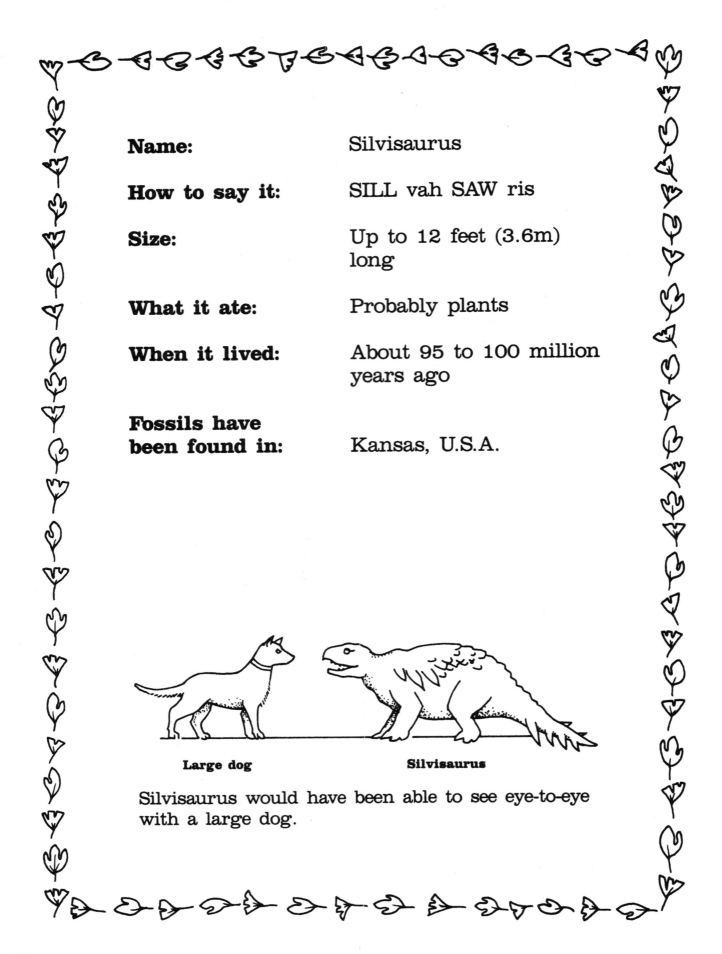

Large dog   **Silvisaurus**

Silvisaurus would have been able to see eye-to-eye with a large dog.

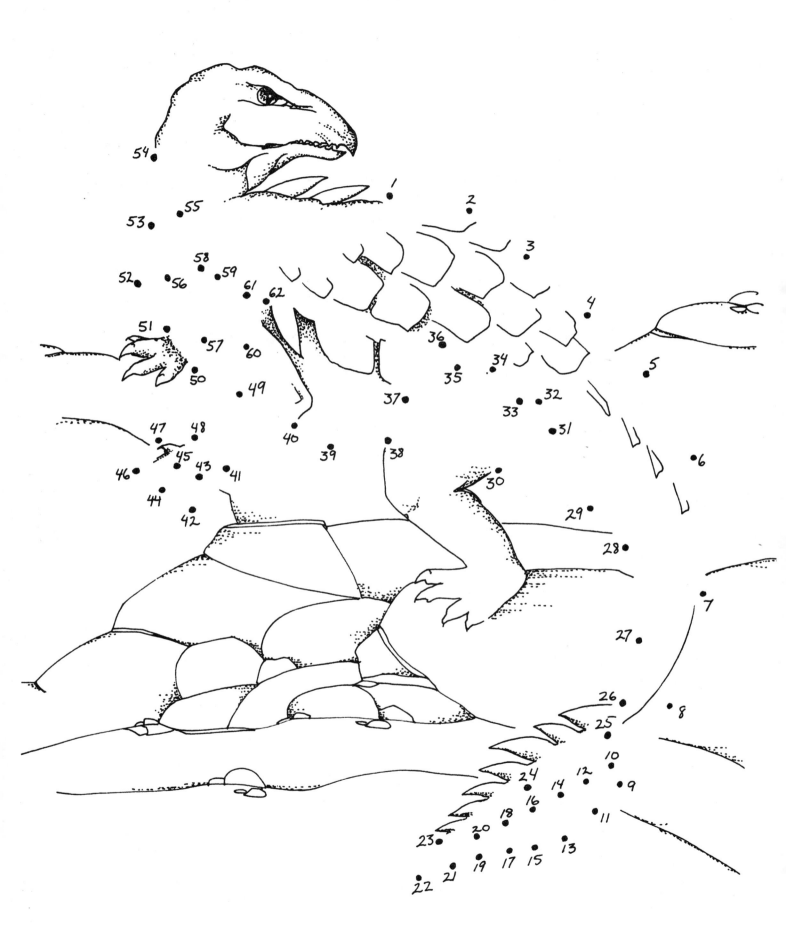

69

Name:	Spinosaurus
How to say it:	SPY no SAW ris
Size:	Up to 50 feet (1.5m) long
What it ate:	Meat
When it lived:	About 110 million years ago
Fossils have been found in:	Egypt

The original fossils of Spinosaurus were lost or destroyed in World War II. Scientists hope to find another set of fossils in the future.

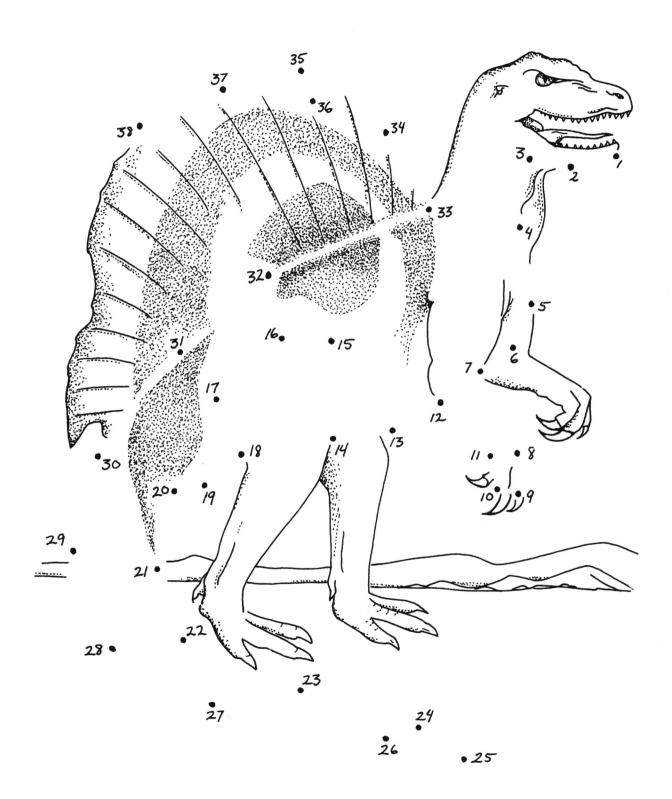

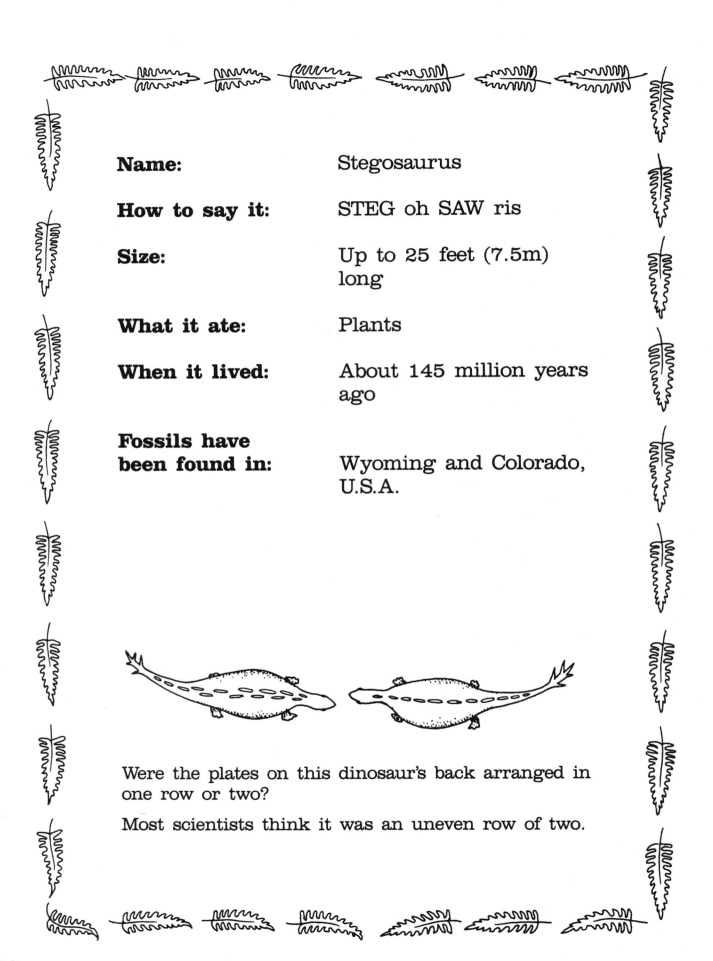

Name:	Stegosaurus
How to say it:	STEG oh SAW ris
Size:	Up to 25 feet (7.5m) long
What it ate:	Plants
When it lived:	About 145 million years ago
Fossils have been found in:	Wyoming and Colorado, U.S.A.

Were the plates on this dinosaur's back arranged in one row or two?

Most scientists think it was an uneven row of two.

Name:	Triceratops
How to say it:	try SAIR atops
Size:	Up to 30 feet (9m) long
	It weighed as much as a modern elephant.
What it ate:	Plants
When it lived:	About 70 million years ago
Fossils have been found in:	Wyoming and Montana, U.S.A. Alberta and Saskatchewan, Canada

Ten different types of Triceratops have been found in the American West.

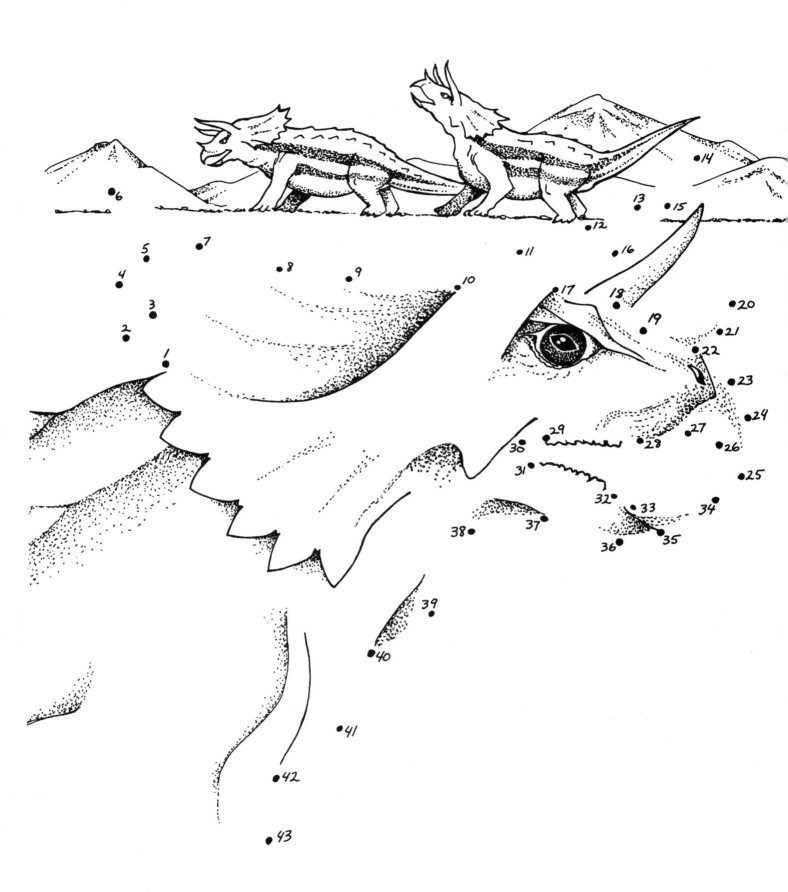

Name:	Tyrannosaurus
How to say it:	ty RAN ah SAW ris
Size:	Up to 50 feet (15m) long About 20 feet (6m) tall
What it ate:	Meat
When it lived:	About 65 to 70 million years ago
Fossils have been found in:	Hell Creek, Montana, U.S.A.

Some scientists think Tyrannosaurus weighed as little as two and a half tons (2.25 tonnes), while others think he might have weighed as much as seven tons (6.3 tonnes).

The largest teeth of Tyrannosaurus were longer than a ball-point pen.

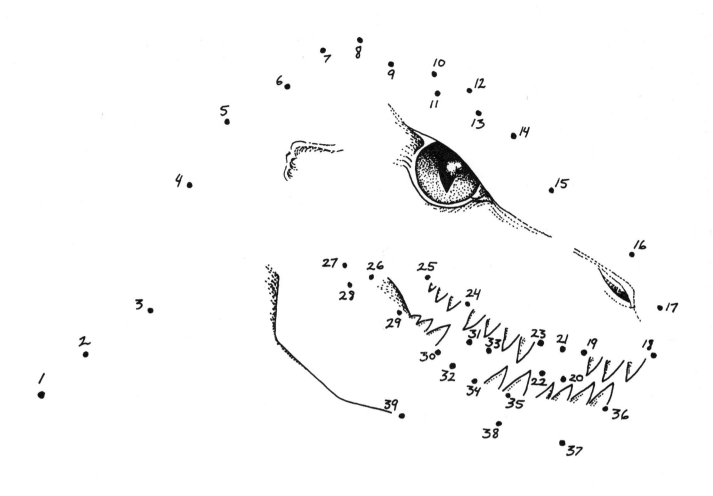
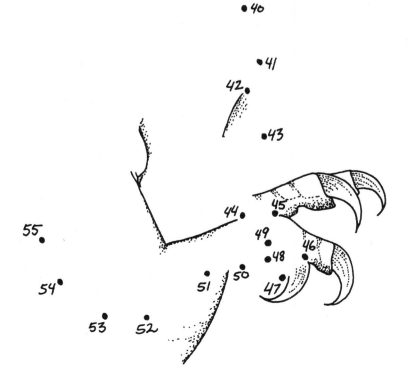

Extinct Animals

DOT-TO-DOT

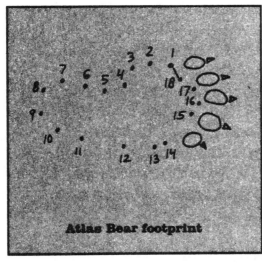

Atlas Bear footprint

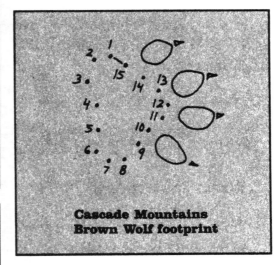

Cascade Mountains
Brown Wolf footprint

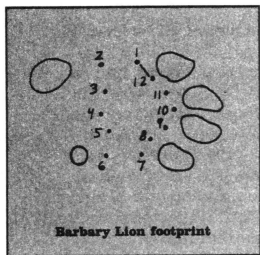

Barbary Lion footprint

Susan Baumgart

Illustrated by Richard Salvucci

Atlas Bear

Pronounced:	AT-lus Bear
Where it lived:	North Africa
Size:	5–8 feet (1.7–2.5m) long, and about 3–4 feet (.9–1.2m) tall. It weighed between 130 and 440 pounds (60–200kg).
What it ate:	Probably mostly plants, fruits, and nuts, some fish, and now and then small animals, such as mice and squirrels
When last seen:	1870

The Atlas Bear once roamed all of North Africa, but now it is gone. What happened?

A few thousand years ago, North Africa had beautiful forests. When the Romans took over, they cut down the trees to build ships and to clear space for sheep and goats. Once the sandy soil was no longer protected by trees, the area became a desert—the great Sahara Desert! Bears couldn't live in a desert—they needed the plants and shelter of the forest. Their last home was in the Atlas Mountains in Morocco, where hunters killed them for sport. No one has reported seeing them for over 100 years.

Color:	Black and dark brown

Barbary Lion

Pronounced: BAR-bar-ee Lion

Where it lived: North Africa

Size: 5½ to 8½ feet (1.7 to 2.5m) long. Its height at the shoulder was about 4 feet (1.2m). It weighed between 330 and 400 pounds (120 and 180kg).

What it ate: Large animals, such as deer, buffalo, and antelope—living or dead

When last seen: 1922

The Barbary Lion was one of the largest lions ever. It lived in North Africa before the forest was cut down. When the land became a desert, many lions died because they didn't have the food and shelter they needed.

Hundreds of lions were also killed by the Romans in ancient times. When Christians were "fed to the lions" in huge stadiums, the lions were killed, too.

In addition, as the human population grew in North Africa, more and more lions were killed by farmers protecting their flocks. With the coming of guns, hunters and farmers "won" over the lives of lions.

Color: Yellowish tan with creamy area below nose and on chin

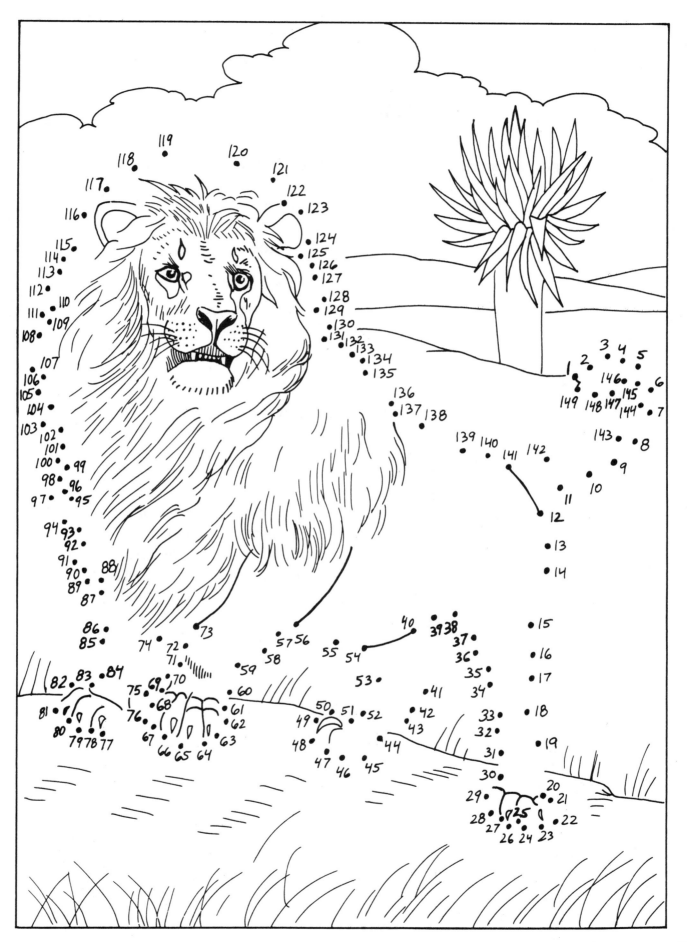

Caribbean Monk Seal

Pronounced:	kuh-RIB-ee-un Monk Seal
Where it lived:	Caribbean Sea
Size:	6½ to 8 feet (2 to 2.4m) long
What it ate:	Probably fish, octopus, and shellfish
When last seen:	1949

The first animal Christopher Columbus wrote about in his journal when he got to the New World was the Caribbean Monk Seal. His crewmen killed eight of them. Very soon, the large seal was being hunted for its oil and fur. The last group of Caribbean Monk Seals was seen in 1911 swimming off the coast of the Yucatan Peninsula, Mexico. Fishermen slaughtered all 200 of them. A few individuals were sighted after that, the last being near Jamaica in 1949. Scientists searched for them in 1972 and 1980, but found none.

Color:	Black, with grey around the eyes and mouth

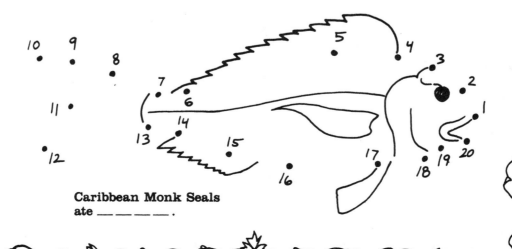

Caribbean Monk Seals
ate _ _ _ _ _ _ .

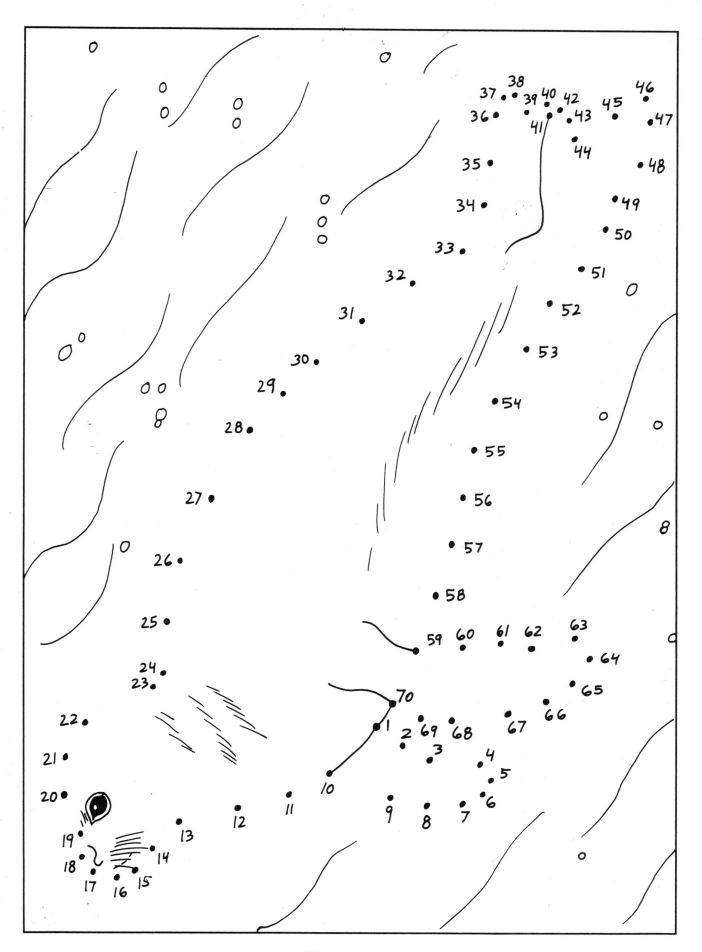

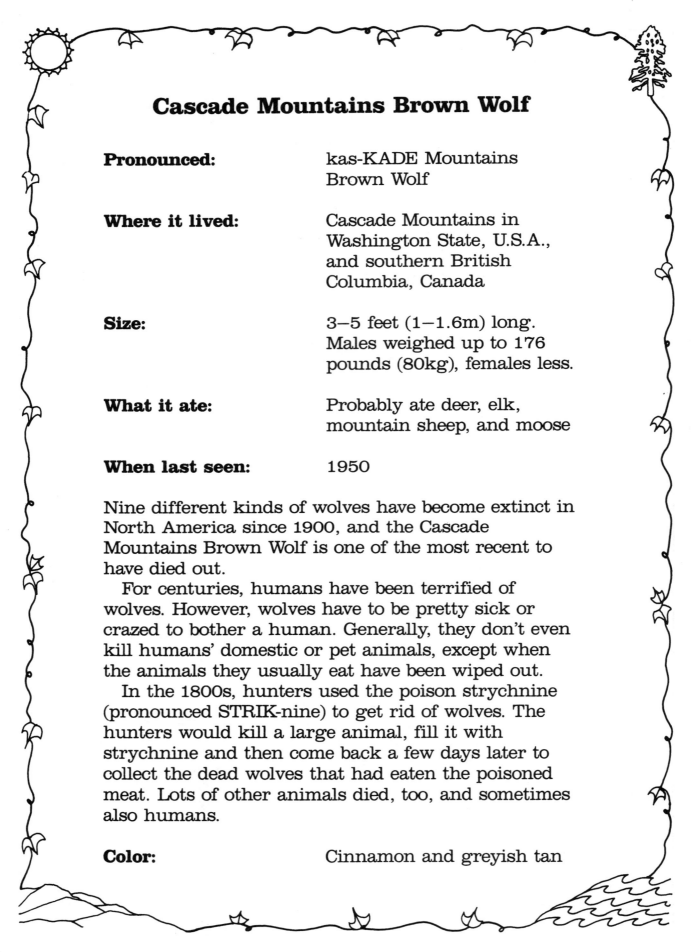

Cascade Mountains Brown Wolf

Pronounced: kas-KADE Mountains Brown Wolf

Where it lived: Cascade Mountains in Washington State, U.S.A., and southern British Columbia, Canada

Size: 3–5 feet (1–1.6m) long. Males weighed up to 176 pounds (80kg), females less.

What it ate: Probably ate deer, elk, mountain sheep, and moose

When last seen: 1950

Nine different kinds of wolves have become extinct in North America since 1900, and the Cascade Mountains Brown Wolf is one of the most recent to have died out.

For centuries, humans have been terrified of wolves. However, wolves have to be pretty sick or crazed to bother a human. Generally, they don't even kill humans' domestic or pet animals, except when the animals they usually eat have been wiped out.

In the 1800s, hunters used the poison strychnine (pronounced STRIK-nine) to get rid of wolves. The hunters would kill a large animal, fill it with strychnine and then come back a few days later to collect the dead wolves that had eaten the poisoned meat. Lots of other animals died, too, and sometimes also humans.

Color: Cinnamon and greyish tan

Cuban Red Macaw

Pronounced: KEW-bun Red mah-KAW

Where it lived: Island of Cuba, south of Florida in the Caribbean Sea

Size: About 20 inches (51cm) long

What it ate: Nuts, fruit, seeds

When last seen: 1864

When Columbus returned from America, he brought home to Europe some brightly colored birds that were easily tamed. They became very popular. People would collect or sell them. The beautiful red macaw from Cuba was one of these birds.

The red macaw nested in the holes and notches of palm trees. The usual way to catch them was to chop down the tree in which the birds were nesting in hopes of capturing some undamaged babies. This is still the way birds are obtained for the pet trade in South America. Because so many animals are killed to get just one live, unhurt baby, some countries, like the U.S., have made it illegal to buy or sell birds from South America.

Color: Red head, breast, and legs; yellow back of the neck; brilliant blue wings and tail

Macaws eat _ _ _ _ _ _ , **nuts, and seeds.**

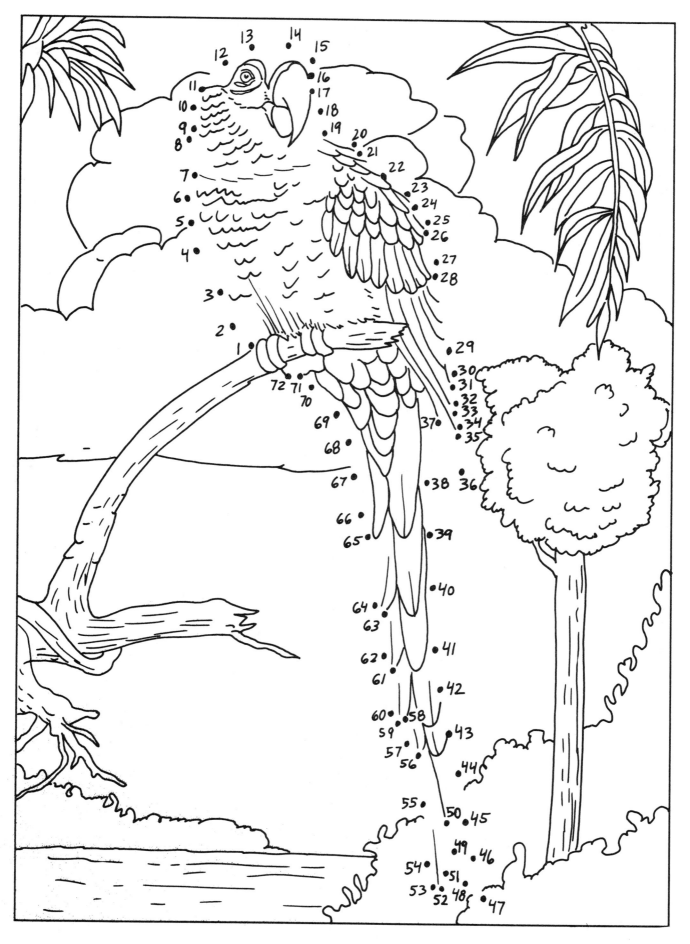

Dodo

Pronounced:	DO-do
Where it lived:	Island of Mauritius, east of Africa
Size:	Up to 3½ feet (1m) tall. It weighed about 50 pounds (22kg).
What it ate:	Low-growing plants, seeds, fallen fruit
When last seen:	1681

Dodos were large doves that couldn't fly. Until European sailors arrived in Mauritius, these gentle birds had no enemies. They would walk right up to visiting seamen, who would club them for sport and food.

When Dutch settlers came to the island in 1644, most of the birds were captured and eaten, or sold to sailors on passing ships. The settlers' dogs wiped out all the remaining adult Dodos, while cats, monkeys, pigs, and rats rooted out eggs and chicks.

When we call someone a dodo today, we mean to call them stupid, but were Dodos really stupid? People may have thought so just because Dodos were gentle and didn't know how to defend themselves.

Color:	Shades of brown and grey, with a white plume on the tail and yellowish feet

Eastern Bison
(Buffalo)

Pronounced: Eastern BY-son

Where it lived: East of the Mississippi
River, from the Great Lakes
down through Virginia,
U.S.A.

Size: To 12 feet (3.5m) long.
It probably weighed
about 800—1100 pounds
(350—500 kg).

What it ate: Grass and tender shoots

When last seen: 1825 in West Virginia

Originally, there were four kinds of bison in the
U.S.A. They lived in large herds—sometimes over a
million animals. Two kinds of bison are completely
gone, one of them being the Eastern Bison, the
largest of all.

Native Americans got food, clothing, and shelter
from bisons (buffaloes), using every part of the
animal and taking a life only when it was really
necessary. But when European settlers arrived, they
killed animals wastefully, selling their skins and
leaving most of the rest of the body to rot. Some
people set fire to the plants the bison ate, driving
away all animals, large and small, and then chased
and shot them for "fun."

Color: Black, with grizzly white
hairs around nose and eyes

Eastern Elk
(Wapiti)

Pronounced: (wah-PEE-tee)

Where it lived: Eastern plains of Canada and the U.S.

Size: 6–9 feet (1.8–2.6m) long. Its height at the shoulder was about 2½ to 5 feet (.75 to 1.5m). It weighed about 165 to 750 pounds (75–340kg).

What it ate: Grass and leafy plants

When last seen: 1877

The Eastern Elk was as important to Native Americans as the buffalo. It provided meat, leather, and a prized ornament, the upper canine teeth. Those teeth were part of the elk's undoing.

The Native Americans decorated their robes with elks' teeth. Sometimes they carved imitation teeth out of bone and wore those instead. When white men became interested in the teeth, however, they would not accept fake ones. The Order of the Elks, an organization founded to do good deeds for the community, created such a demand for the teeth as a sign of their brotherhood that they speeded up the extinction of the Eastern Elk!

Color: Tan and greyish tan, with long black hairs circling the neck and on the belly; blackish brown legs

Elephant Bird

Where it lived: Madagascar

Size: Up to 10 feet (3m) tall, and
                             weighing about 1,100
                             pounds (500kg)

What it ate: Probably plants, fruit, small
                             mammals, and dead animals

When last seen: 1700

As far as we know, the Elephant Bird was the largest
bird ever. Its eggs were nearly a foot across—three
times the size of the eggs of the largest dinosaurs.
One egg, cooked, could serve 75 people.

The Elephant Bird had thick, strong legs and
heavy-duty claws. Its body was covered with feathers
that looked like bristly hair. The bird didn't fly—it
ran. Other animals didn't want to mess with it,
because it was so big. It was shy, though, hiding
from people in the swampy jungle. But wet forest
was shrinking in Madagascar, partially because
rainfall was decreasing, and partly because humans
were chopping down the forest. Then, when people
stole its eggs and killed the big birds with guns,
axes, and fire, the last Elephant Birds were gone.

Color: Brown—darker on the top,
                             lightest at the throat

The Elephant Bird
probably scratched
in the dirt for food
with its

_ _ _ _ _ _ .

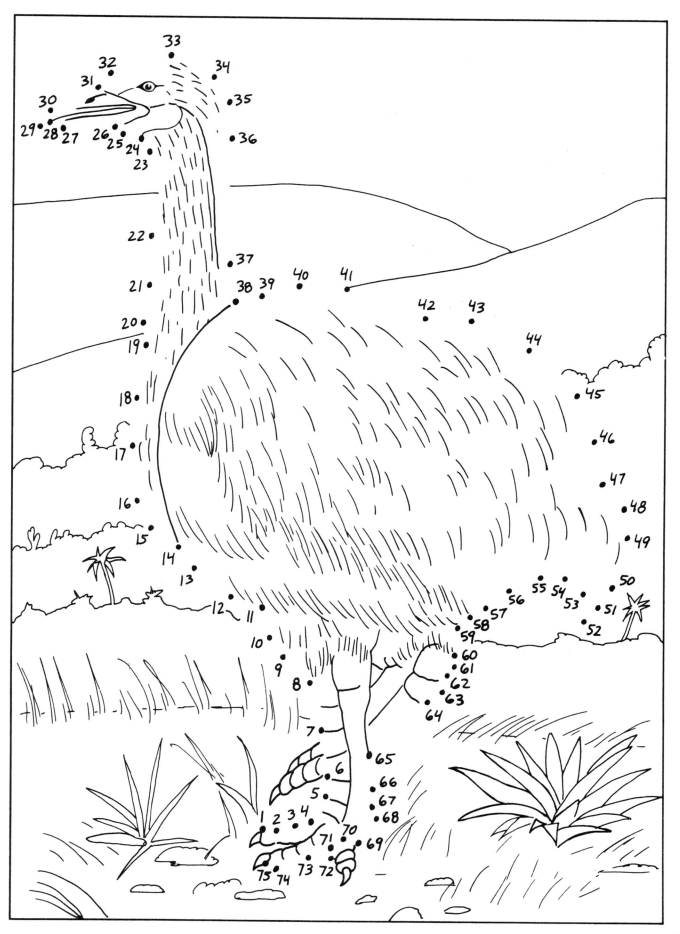

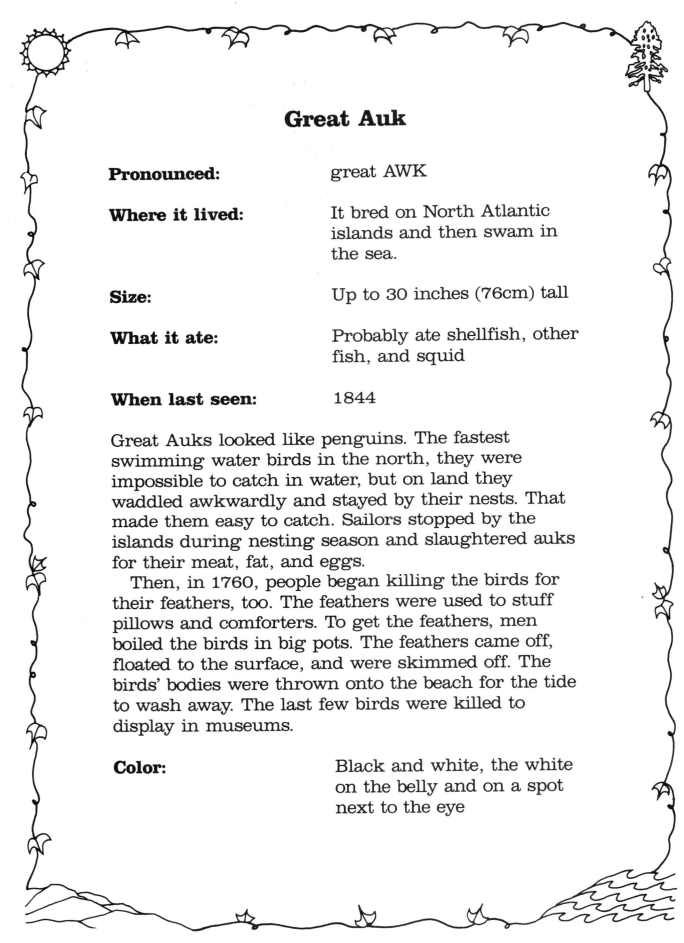

Great Auk

Pronounced: great AWK

Where it lived: It bred on North Atlantic islands and then swam in the sea.

Size: Up to 30 inches (76cm) tall

What it ate: Probably ate shellfish, other fish, and squid

When last seen: 1844

Great Auks looked like penguins. The fastest swimming water birds in the north, they were impossible to catch in water, but on land they waddled awkwardly and stayed by their nests. That made them easy to catch. Sailors stopped by the islands during nesting season and slaughtered auks for their meat, fat, and eggs.

Then, in 1760, people began killing the birds for their feathers, too. The feathers were used to stuff pillows and comforters. To get the feathers, men boiled the birds in big pots. The feathers came off, floated to the surface, and were skimmed off. The birds' bodies were thrown onto the beach for the tide to wash away. The last few birds were killed to display in museums.

Color: Black and white, the white on the belly and on a spot next to the eye

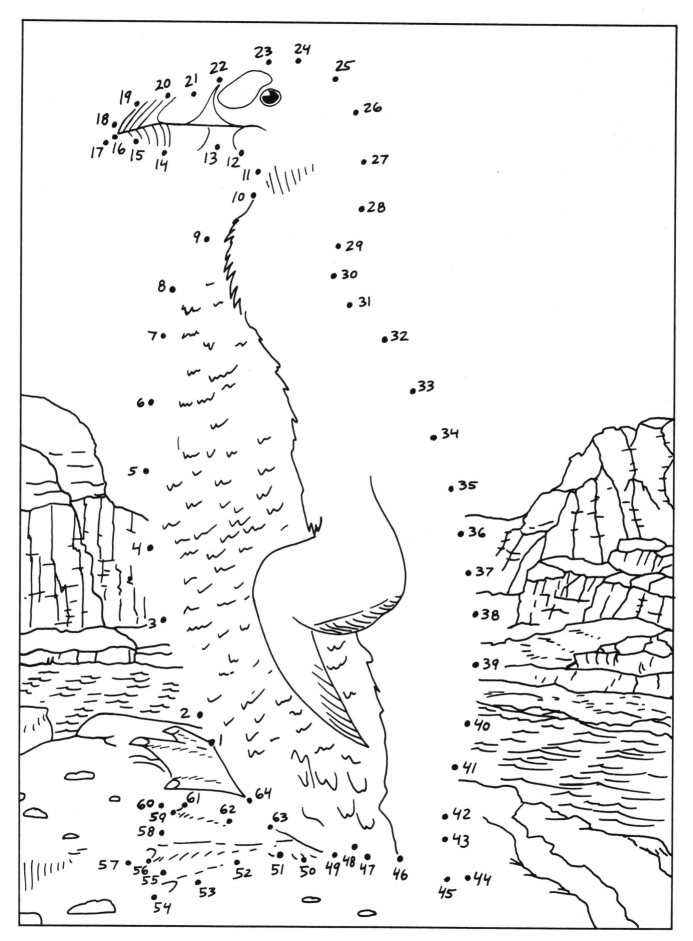

Heath Hen

Where it lived: East of the Rocky Mountains in the U.S.A.

Size: 15—18 inches (38—45cm) long

What it ate: Leafy plants, insects, fruit, seeds, and acorns

When last seen: 1932

When the colonists first came to America, Heath Hens were so plentiful that some families in Boston asked their cooks not to serve the bird more than a few times a week! But the settlers turned the birds' brushy home into farmland, and dogs and cats killed the hens and their young. Hunters shot the birds while they sat on their nests, which got rid of the next generation at the same time.

By 1830, the only Heath Hens left lived on Martha's Vineyard, an island off the coast of Massachusetts, where no one was allowed to hunt them. Then a fire raced across the island during nesting season, and many of the hens wouldn't leave their young. The few survivors were eaten by hawks or died as a result of a severe winter and disease.

Color: Shades of brown and cream

Males of the species made loud, booming _____ with their round air sacks.

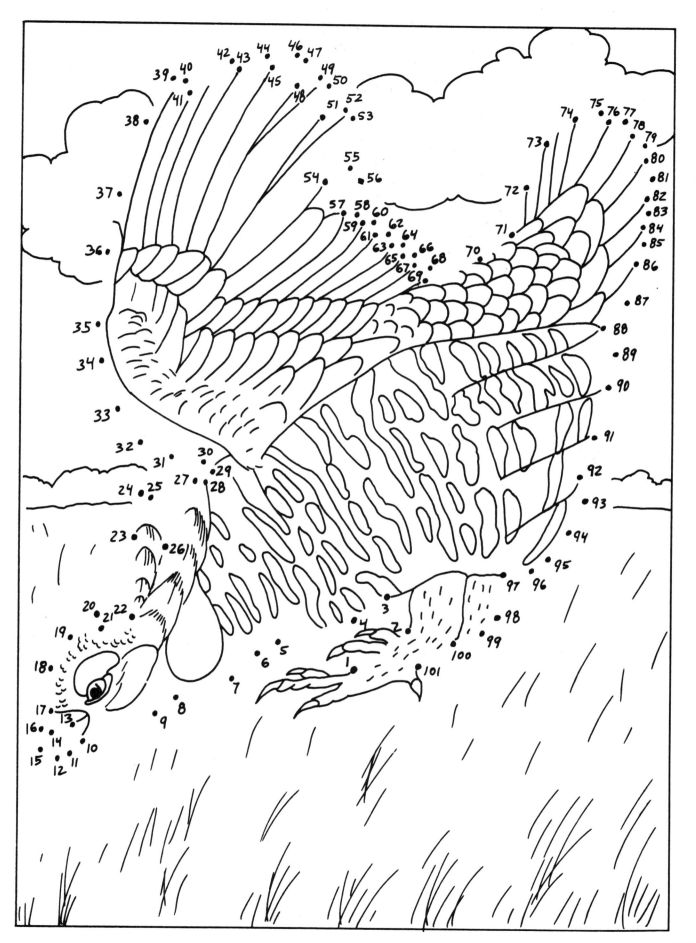

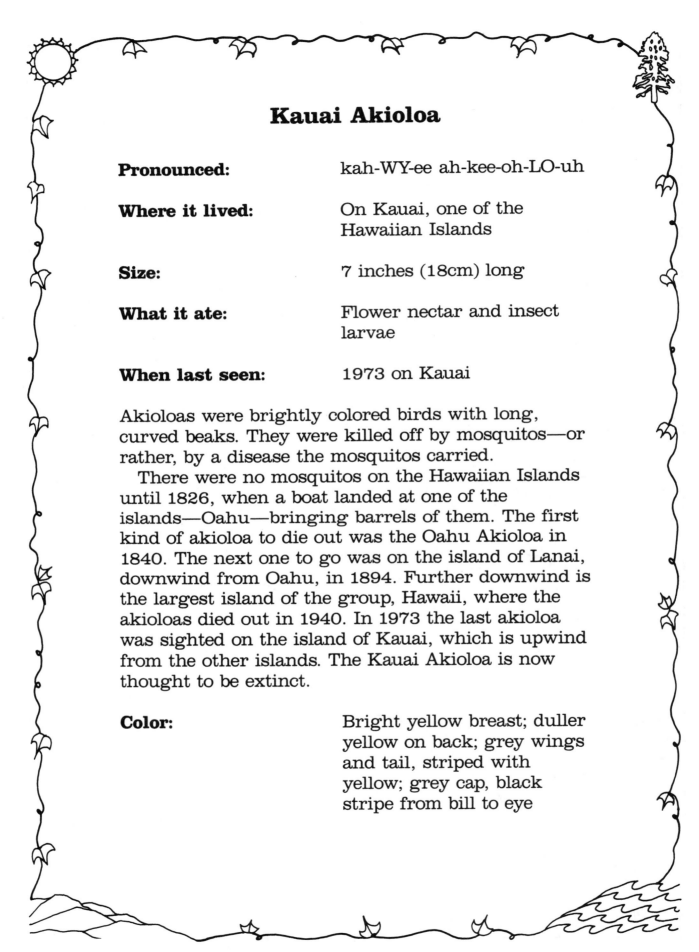

Kauai Akioloa

Pronounced: kah-WY-ee ah-kee-oh-LO-uh

Where it lived: On Kauai, one of the Hawaiian Islands

Size: 7 inches (18cm) long

What it ate: Flower nectar and insect larvae

When last seen: 1973 on Kauai

Akioloas were brightly colored birds with long, curved beaks. They were killed off by mosquitos—or rather, by a disease the mosquitos carried.

There were no mosquitos on the Hawaiian Islands until 1826, when a boat landed at one of the islands—Oahu—bringing barrels of them. The first kind of akioloa to die out was the Oahu Akioloa in 1840. The next one to go was on the island of Lanai, downwind from Oahu, in 1894. Further downwind is the largest island of the group, Hawaii, where the akioloas died out in 1940. In 1973 the last akioloa was sighted on the island of Kauai, which is upwind from the other islands. The Kauai Akioloa is now thought to be extinct.

Color: Bright yellow breast; duller yellow on back; grey wings and tail, striped with yellow; grey cap, black stripe from bill to eye

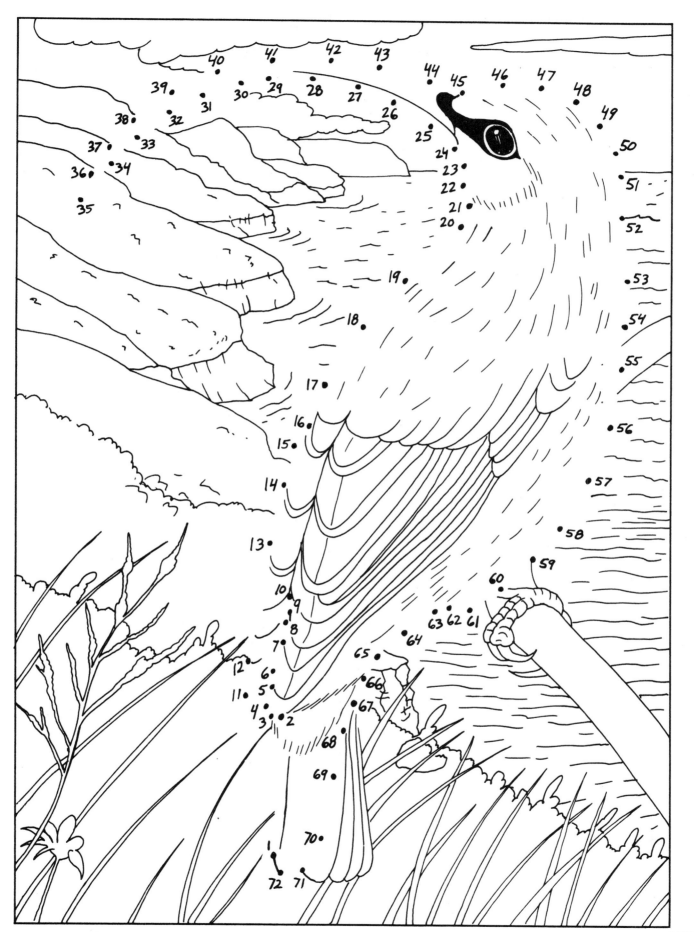

Mexican Silver Grizzly Bear

Where it lived: Mexico and in the southwestern U.S.A.

Size: 5½–9½ feet (1.7–2.8m) long. Its height at the shoulder was from 3–5 feet (.9–1.5m). It weighed between 220 and 660 pounds (100 and 300kg).

What it ate: Probably mostly plants, fruits, berries, and nuts, some fish, and now and then small animals, such as mice and squirrels.

When last seen: 1970

By the 1930s, the Mexican Silver Grizzly Bear had been hunted, trapped, and poisoned so widely that it was gone from the United States. It could still be found in Mexico, though, where it was the largest animal ever seen.

By 1962, only about 30 grizzlies were left in Mexico, in an isolated mountain range. Ranchers succeeded in killing them by 1964. In 1969, a group of grizzlies were spotted in another Mexican mountain range, but they haven't been seen since.

Color: Black legs, nose, lips, ears, and around the eyes; reddish brown body and face; silvery white long hairs that reached beyond the main brown coat

105

Passenger Pigeon

Where it lived: North America, mostly in the eastern U.S. and Canada

Size: About 12 inches (30cm) long

What it ate: Nuts, fruits, seeds, insects, and worms

When last seen: 1914

Passenger Pigeons flew in flocks a mile wide. It took as long as three hours for them to pass overhead, travelling at 60 miles (96km) an hour! They would darken the sun like a cloud. There were probably one to two billion birds in just one flock! When settlers came to America, Passenger Pigeons were the most common birds in the world. Within 50 years, they were hunted to extinction. Adult birds provided good, cheap meat. Babies were a tender delicacy. Some of the pigeons' insides and even their dung were sold for medical cures. Feathers were used for pillows and quilts.

The last wild bird was shot in 1907. The last zoo pigeon died in 1914.

Color: Blue head, back wings, and tail; orange breast fading to creamy undersides

The Passenger Pigeon fed on farmers' seeds, such as oats, and wild seeds, like this

— — — — — .

106

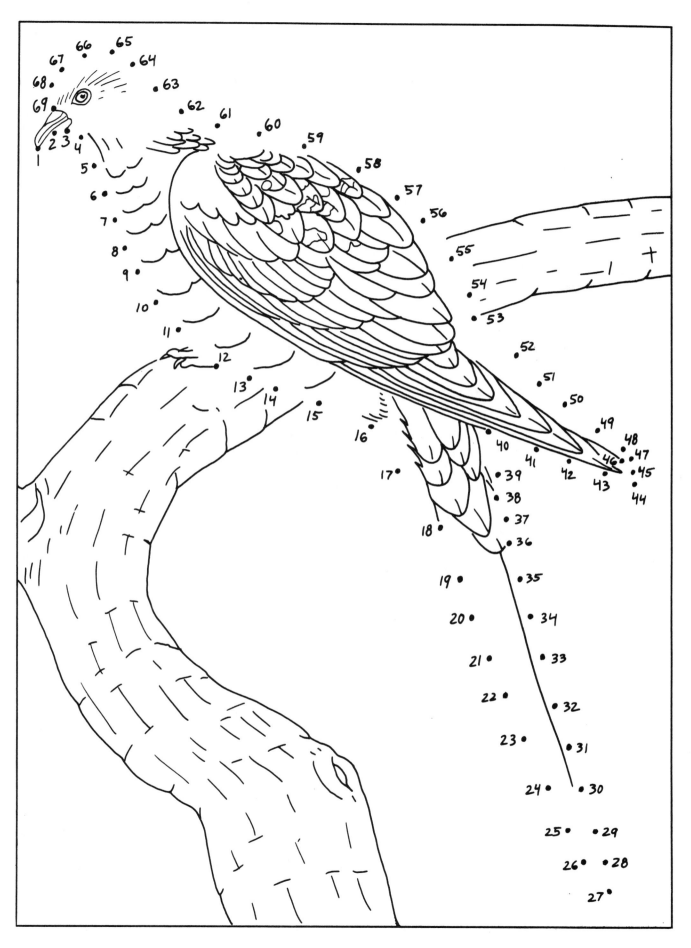

Quelili

Pronounced:	kay-LEE-lee
Where it lived:	Guadalupe Island, 140 miles (225km) west of Baja California
Size:	22 inches (54cm) tall
What it ate:	Small birds, mice, worms, and dead animals
When last seen:	1900

Settlers brought goats to Guadalupe Island in the early 1700s. The goats multiplied, devouring all the plants on the island. When the plants were gone, the goats started to die off. The herders probably saw the Quelili, a large hawk, eating the dead and dying goats, and imagined that it killed them. They slaughtered the hawks, thinking they were pests.

When scientists expressed interest in the Quelili, the herders captured most of the remaining birds and sold them on the mainland. When only one small flock was left, a scientist went to the island, shot the quelilis, and took them home to be stuffed.

Color:	Mottled brown, with a white face and dark brown cap

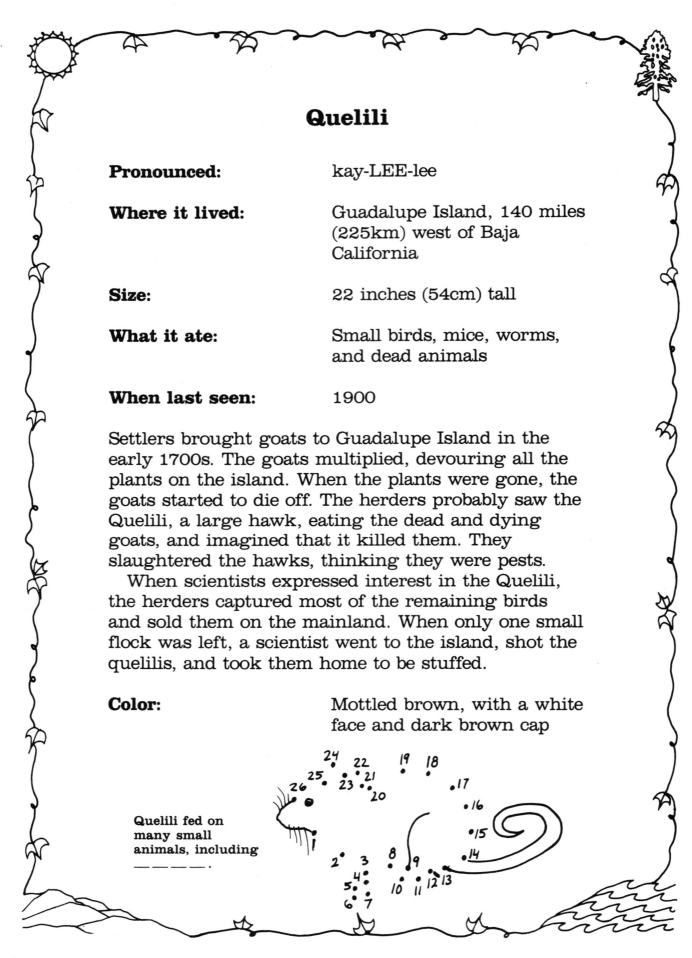

Quelili fed on many small animals, including _____ .

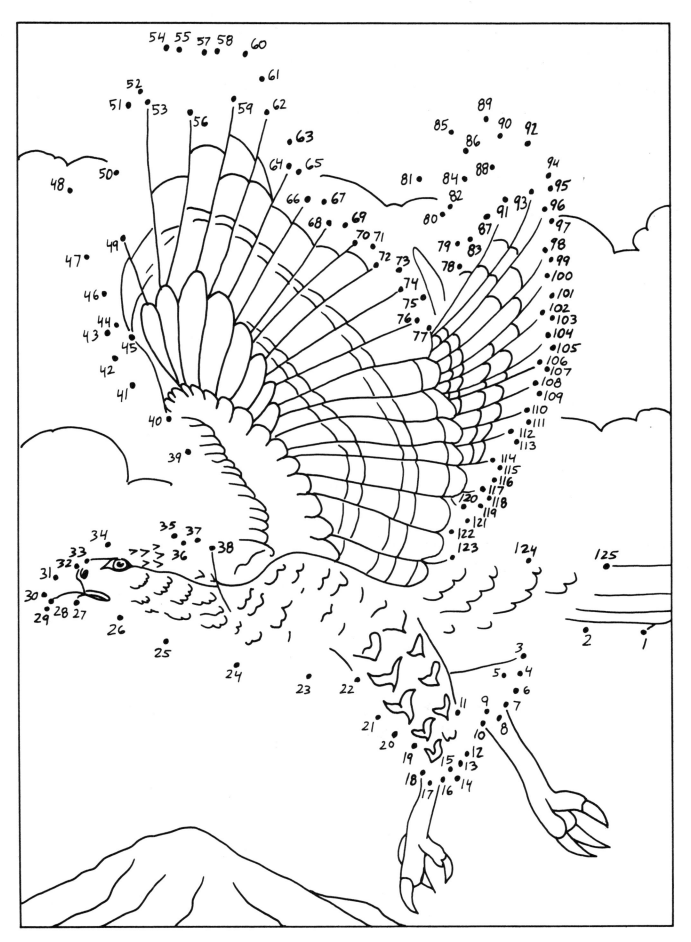

Rodriguez Greater Tortoise

Pronounced:
rah-DREE-gez greater TOR-tus

Where it lived:
In the Mascarene Islands, which lie east of Madagascar in the Indian Ocean

Size:
100 pounds (45kg) and about as long as a human's arm

What it ate:
Leafy plants and fruit

When last seen:
1800

When sailors first saw the Rodriguez Greater Tortoise, the Mascarene Islands were covered with them. One seaman wrote that they lived in flocks of two to three thousand! He said they gathered in shady places at the end of the day, huddling so close that the area seemed paved with their shells.

Unfortunately for the tortoises, their meat tasted good. Less than 100 years after the seaman published his journal, all of them were gone. Ships sailing by killed hundreds of tortoises at a time. Then, when people settled the islands, they brought pigs and rats with them, who destroyed the tortoises' eggs. Rodriguez Greater Tortoises—and most other large tortoises that used to live on earth—were no match for "civilization."

Color:
Mostly brown, with some brownish grey on the skin

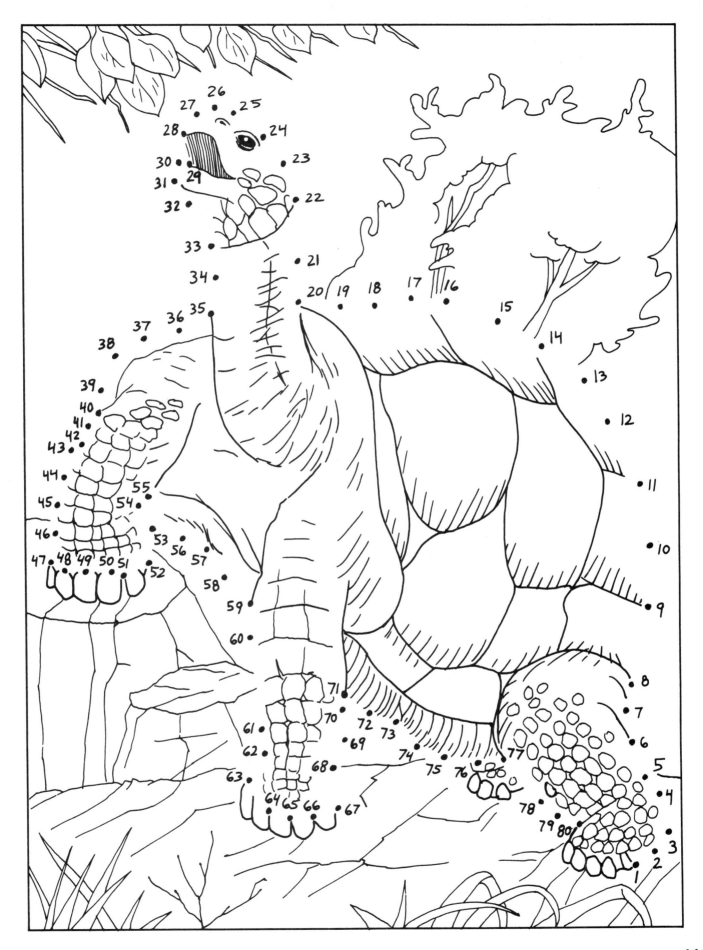

111

Round Island Boa

Pronounced: Round Island BO-uh

Where it lived: Round Island, one of the Mascarene Islands, east of Madagascar, a larger island that lies east of Africa

Size: About 4 feet (1.2m) long

What it ate: Small birds and mammals

When last seen: 1980

Round Island is a tiny volcanic land poking out of the Indian Ocean. It is only a little bigger than half a square mile across (1.5sq km). Many animals and plants that live there are found nowhere else on earth. The Round Island Boa was one of these unique creatures. It would slither through the bushes and catch small animals, killing them by squeezing them until they couldn't breathe.

In 1844, people brought rabbits and goats to the island. These animals ate the plants down to the ground, even gobbling up young seedlings so nothing new could grow. The loose soil, exposed to heavy rains, turned to mud. Gullies formed up to 30 feet (9m) deep—deep enough to cover a two- or three-story house! With the destruction of their habitat, all the Round Island Boas died.

Color: Shades of brown and tan

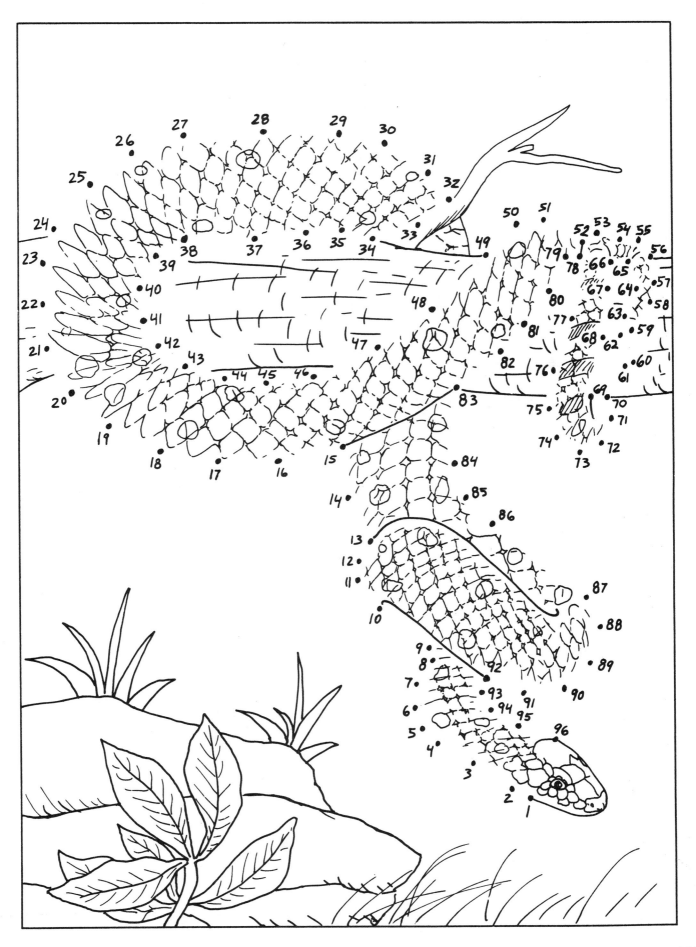

Shortnose Sucker

Where it lived: Oregon, U.S.A.

Size: About 12–20 inches (30–50cm) long

What it ate: Tiny animals and plants that float in the water or coat rocks on the bottom of rivers or lakes

When last seen: 1960

The Shortnose Sucker, a fish that lived in Klamath Lake, was the main food of the Klamath Indians. They ate it both fresh and dried. Once a year, at mating season, the fish swam up two rivers that poured into the lake. There they laid their eggs.

The Shortnose Sucker disappeared when humans built dams on these two rivers. With the route to their spawning grounds blocked, the Shortnose Suckers did not produce baby fish. Eventually, all the fish were either caught or died of old age. They were last seen in Klamath Lake in 1960, though one scientist reported finding them in a man-made lake in 1975.

Color: Grey above the red midline, white below; pinkish white fins; brown cheeks

This fish was named for its stubby _____ .

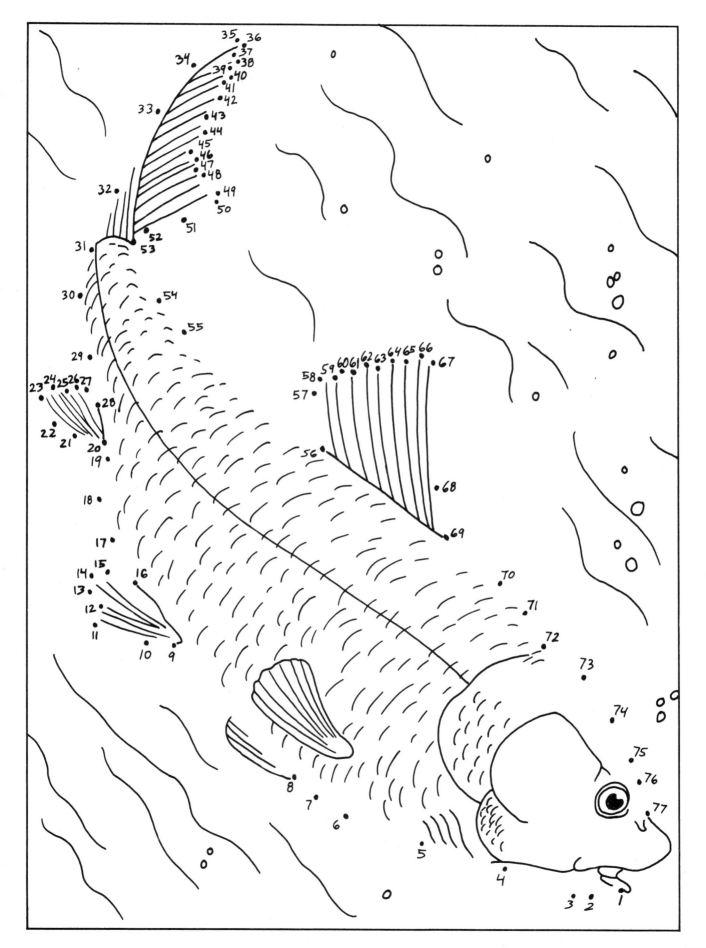

Syrian Onager

Pronounced: SEAR-ee-un AH-nuh-jer

Where it lived: Middle East—Syria, Palestine, Arabia, Mesopotamia

Size: 6½ to 8½ feet (2 to 2.5m) long, and 3½ to 5½ feet (1−1.4m) high at the shoulder, it weighed between 440 and 570 pounds (200 and 260kg).

What it ate: Grasses and other desert plants

When last seen: 1930

The Syrian Onager was a shy, small donkey. It travelled in herds and could survive in the driest, roughest deserts. It was never tamed and made to carry loads the way its African relatives were. Arabs hunted the Syrian Onager for food.

During World War I, the home of the Syrian Onager was overrun with soldiers carrying guns. Guns could kill from a distance. Rather than riding camels, people began driving cars. Cars could outrun the freedom-loving wild donkey. Using guns and cars, hunters slaughtered the Syrian Onager. The last one was shot as it walked down to get a drink at an oasis in northern Arabia.

Color: Tan and cream colors. The mane, nose, inside tips of ears and tip of tail were dark brown.

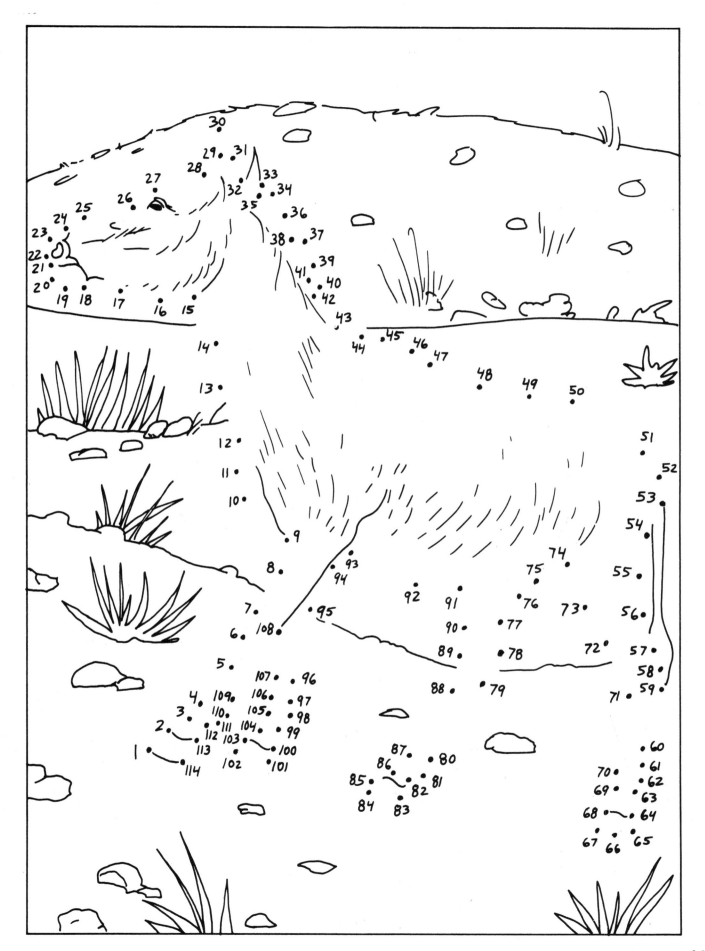

117

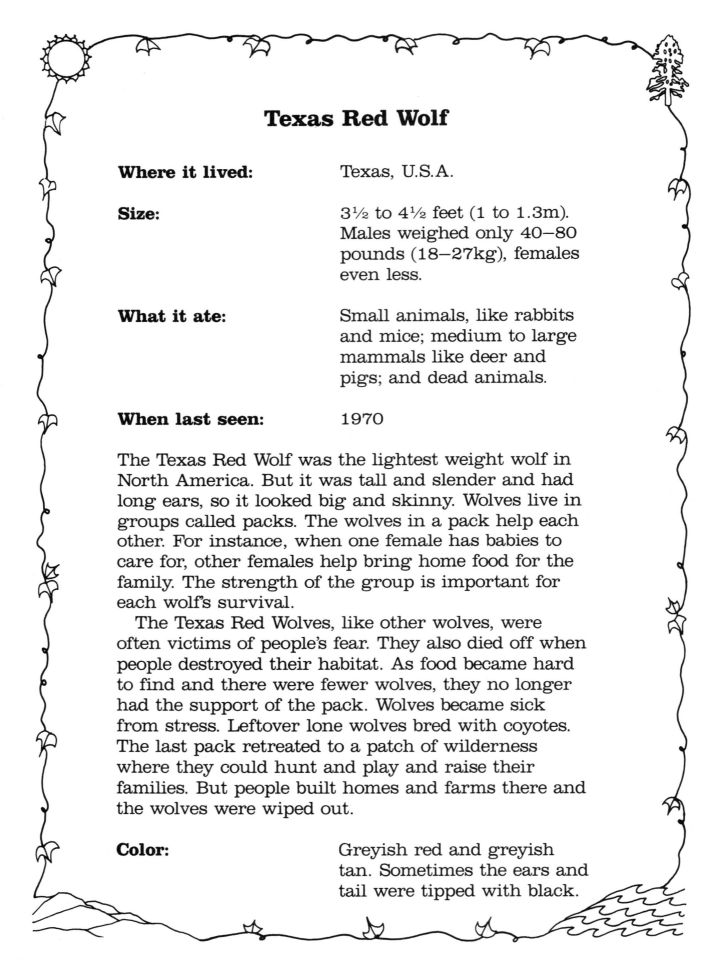

Texas Red Wolf

Where it lived: Texas, U.S.A.

Size: 3½ to 4½ feet (1 to 1.3m). Males weighed only 40–80 pounds (18–27kg), females even less.

What it ate: Small animals, like rabbits and mice; medium to large mammals like deer and pigs; and dead animals.

When last seen: 1970

The Texas Red Wolf was the lightest weight wolf in North America. But it was tall and slender and had long ears, so it looked big and skinny. Wolves live in groups called packs. The wolves in a pack help each other. For instance, when one female has babies to care for, other females help bring home food for the family. The strength of the group is important for each wolf's survival.

The Texas Red Wolves, like other wolves, were often victims of people's fear. They also died off when people destroyed their habitat. As food became hard to find and there were fewer wolves, they no longer had the support of the pack. Wolves became sick from stress. Leftover lone wolves bred with coyotes. The last pack retreated to a patch of wilderness where they could hunt and play and raise their families. But people built homes and farms there and the wolves were wiped out.

Color: Greyish red and greyish tan. Sometimes the ears and tail were tipped with black.

119

ENDANGERED ANIMALS

·········· DOT-TO-DOT ··········

Monica Russo

Name:	African Elephant
Size:	Up to 12 feet (3.6m) long, and about 10 to 13 feet (3—9m) high at the shoulder
Where It Is Endangered:	Africa
Habitat:	Plains, grasslands and scrublands

African Elephants were once quite common, and could be seen travelling in huge herds. But now, an older male with long tusks is a rare sight. The big tusks are really teeth, but they are only used for fighting or defending the young calves. Tusks can grow up to 10 feet (3m) long!

All elephants are vegetarians, eating leaves, grass and tree branches. A large elephant may need as much as 300 pounds of food each day.

The greatest enemy of the African Elephant is man—hunters and ivory poachers have killed thousands of these majestic animals. Many elephants now live in parks and reserves, where they can be protected.

Brownish black, or dark grey

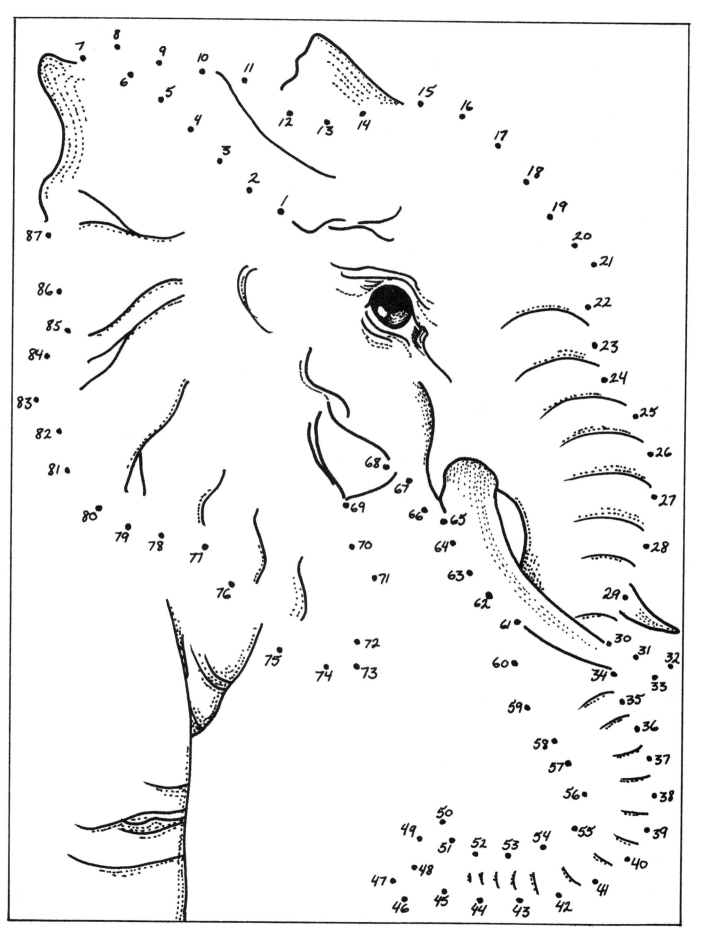

Name:	Arabian Oryx
Size:	About 3 feet (1m) high at the shoulder
Where It Is Endangered:	Yemen, in the Middle East
Habitat:	Open scrubby plains at the edge of the desert

The beautiful Oryx is a type of small antelope. Its graceful horns are about two feet (.6m) long.

It is already extinct as a wild animal! Hunters have killed off every single wild Arabian Oryx. But some zoos and parks have kept the Oryx in captivity, and many of these animals have been born and raised in those zoos. Those young Oryxes are now being released into their natural habitat. Some oryxes born in zoos have been flown back by plane to their desert homes to start new herds again. Now these animals will have to be carefully protected.

Very light tan (almost white) body, chocolate-brown legs, brown patch on face

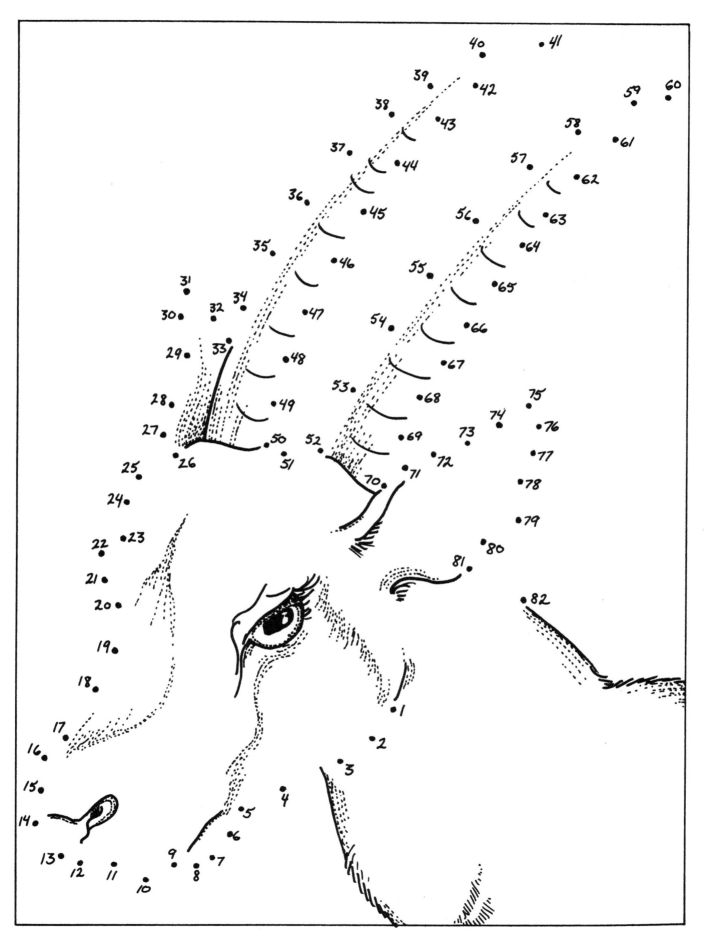

125

Name:	Baiji Dolphin
Size:	About 7 feet (2.1m) long
Where It Is Endangered:	China
Habitat:	Yangtze River

Dolphins are mammals—not fish! They are related to whales and orcas. Most dolphins around the world live in the ocean, and very few live in rivers.

The Baiji Dolphin has a very long nose, or "beak." It eats mostly fish. This rare dolphin may be on the verge of extinction. The Yangtze River is very muddy and polluted, and the dolphins have a hard time finding fish to eat. They are disturbed by the noise of boat motors and injured by fishhooks and propeller blades.

A Chinese conservation group is trying to save Baiji Dolphins by keeping some of them in a protected channel, where they will be safe. But a construction project to build a dam may now spell disaster for the remaining dolphins!

Grey above, white underneath

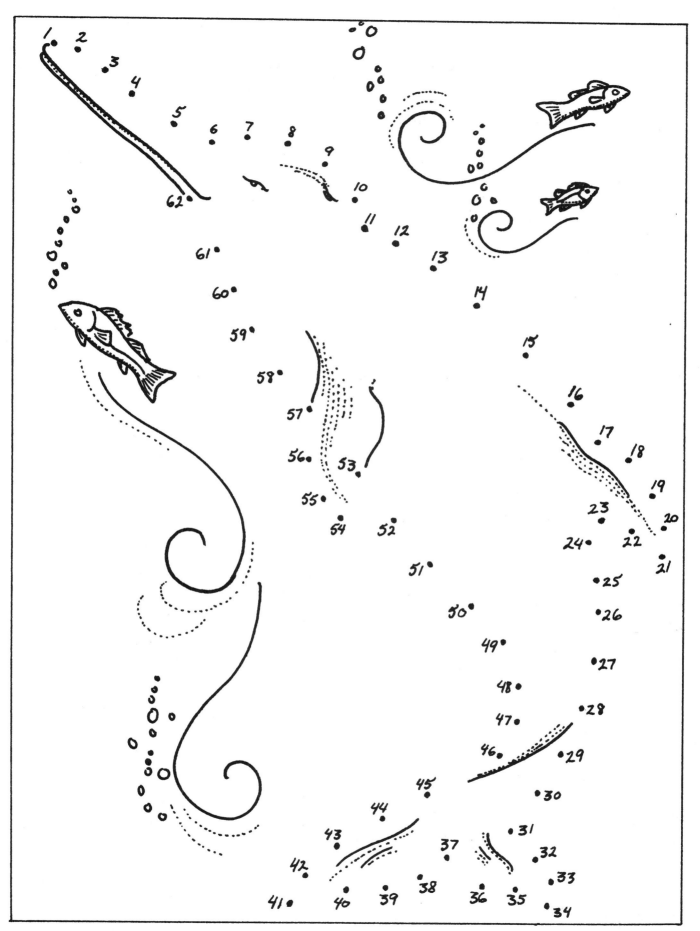

Name:	Bald Eagle
Size:	About 35 inches (1m) long Wingspan: 6 to 8 feet (1.8–2.4m) across
Where It Is Endangered:	United States
Habitat:	Forests near lakes, coastal bays or rivers

The Bald Eagle is the national bird of the United States, and it is protected by federal laws. This eagle grows white head feathers when it's about five years old. Until then, it has dark brown head feathers. The Bald Eagle uses its strong curved claws and beak to catch fish.

Pesticides like DDT have killed many Bald Eagles and prevented their eggs from hatching. Human activity at nesting areas can cause the parent eagles to leave, or not lay eggs.

Snowy white head, yellow beak, yellow eyes. Body feathers are chocolate-brown.

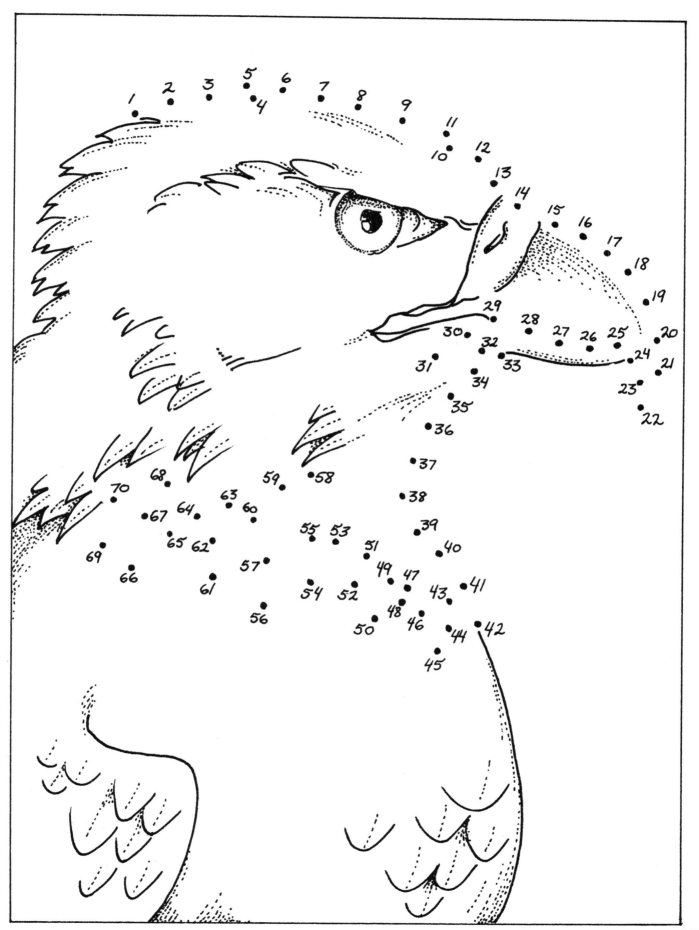

Name:	Bengal Tiger
Size:	About 6 feet (1.8m) long, with a tail about 3 feet (1m) long.
Where It Is Endangered:	India
Habitat:	Jungle forests and grassy fields

The Bengal Tiger is a member of the cat family. Its relatives include the African lion, ocelot, lynx and jaguar.

A fierce hunter, the tiger attacks and kills other animals in the jungle. An adult Bengal Tiger weighs about 500 pounds (225 kg). The wavy stripes on its fur are good camouflage, helping to hide it when it hunts in tall grasses.

The Bengal Tiger is very endangered, and its population keeps declining. Hunters have killed many of these beautiful animals.

Yellow-tan, with black stripes

Name:	Black-Footed Ferret
Size:	About 2 feet (.6m) long
Where It Is Endangered:	Western United States
Habitat:	Prairie grasslands and plains

Ferrets are members of the weasel family, along with skunks and minks. At one time, there were many Black-Footed Ferrets, but now they are rare. Ferrets hunt and eat prairie dogs, which are rodents. The ferrets live in the same areas that prairie dogs live in, and use old prairie dog burrows for their own dens. Prairie dogs were once poisoned in great numbers because they were a nuisance to farmers. Some conservationists believe the poisons might have killed a lot of the Black-Footed Ferrets, too.

Note: Some ferrets sold as pets in pet stores look just like these rare animals, but they are not wild Black-Footed Ferrets!

Yellow-buff body, black mask across face, black feet, black tail-tip

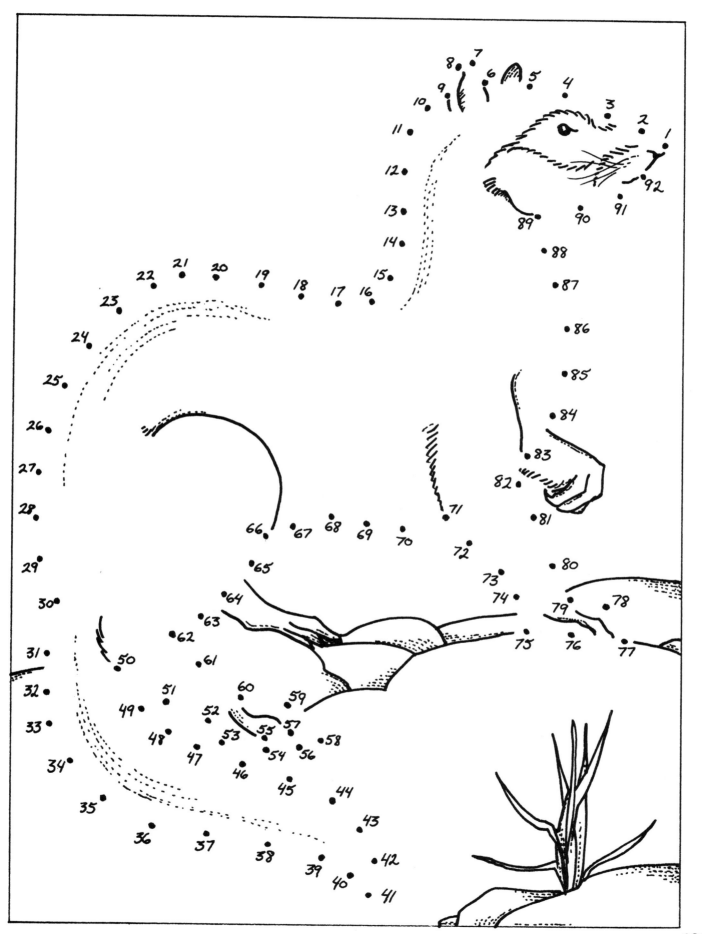

133

Name:	Blue Whale
Size:	About 80 feet (24m) long Record size is about 100 feet (30m) long!
Where It Is Endangered:	All oceans
Habitat:	Oceans, coastal bays and gulfs.

A Blue Whale can dive close to 1,000 feet (300m) deep. A newborn whale is just over 20 feet (6m) long.

Blue Whales don't have teeth. Instead, they have "sifters" called baleen plates, which strain out tiny shrimp-like creatures that the whales eat. The water drains away from the baleen strainers, leaving the whale with a mouthful of food! Thousands of these huge whales were once killed for their oil, but now they are on the U.S. endangered species list and are protected by law.

Dark blue-grey, lighter spots or blotches on the side

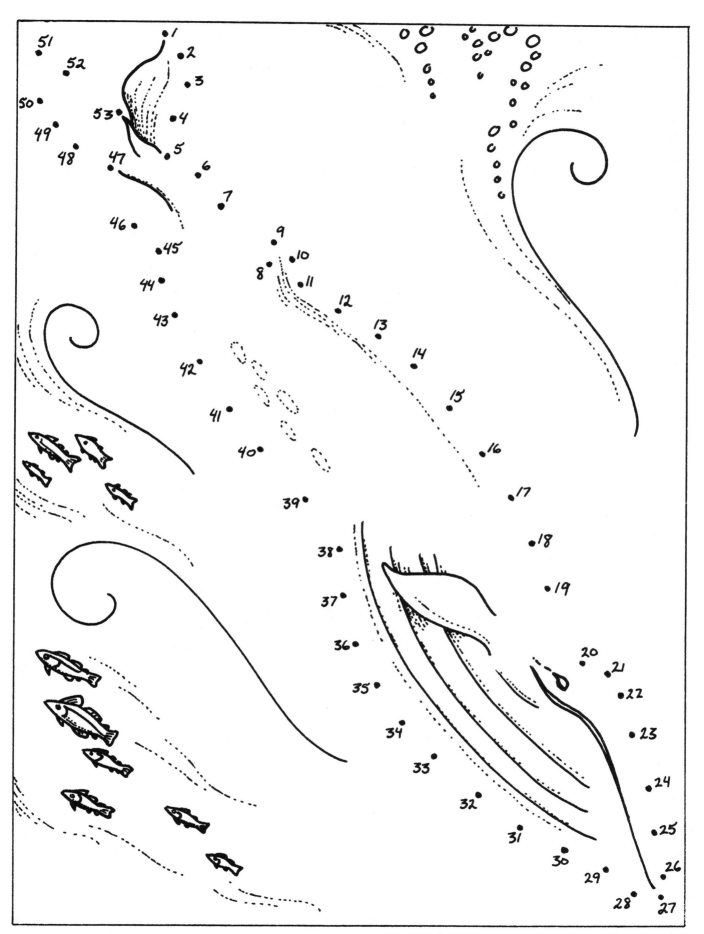

Name:	California Condor
Size:	Wingspan: About 9 to 10 feet (2.7–3m) across (more than twice the span of your outstretched arms!)
Where It Is Endangered:	Southern California, U.S.
Habitat:	Mountains and open grasslands

This huge bird may have an ugly face, but it is magnificent in flight, soaring, gliding and swooping high in the mountains. Condors are scavengers, feeding only on dead animals. But they like to be clean, taking baths in mountain pools and streams!

There are very few Condors left, and most of them are in zoos. The Condor is endangered, because many have been shot by hunters or poisoned, or their nesting sites have been disturbed. Condors only lay one or two eggs—every *other* year!

Shining black feathers, pinkish red neck, yellowish head, red eyes, long silky black feathers around the neck

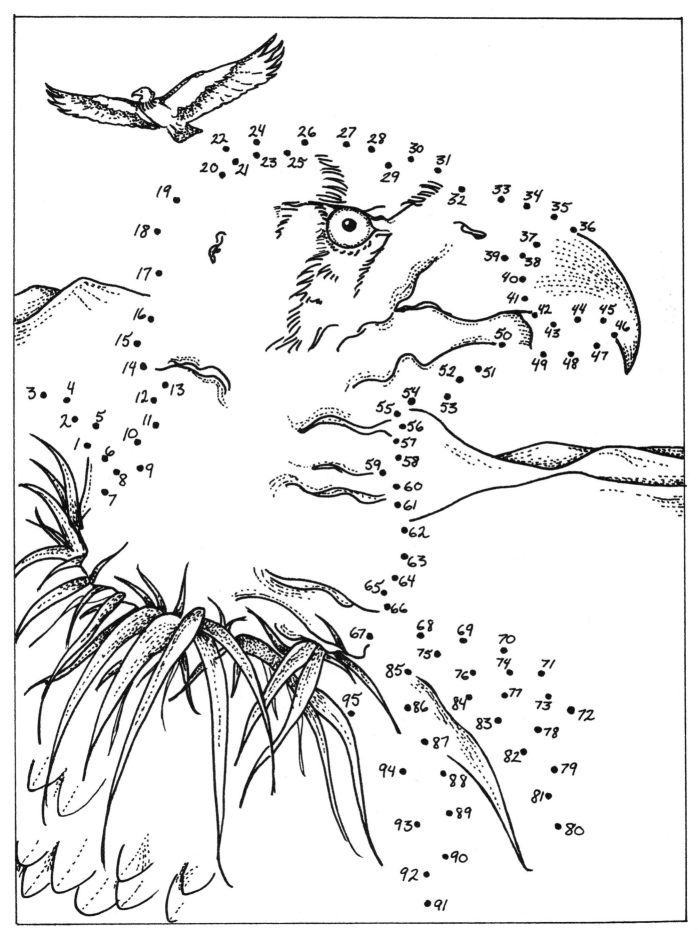

Name:	Cheetah
Size:	About 7 feet (2.1m) long, including the tail
Where It Is Endangered:	Africa, Mideast, India
Habitat:	Open grassy plains

Cheetahs are swift and slender hunters. They eat birds, small animals and larger animals like gazelles. They can run as fast as 75 miles per hour, for a short dash.

Cheetahs once lived in India, but they are probably extinct there now. No one has seen wild Cheetahs in India for a long time. Some Cheetahs are left in Afghanistan, Iran and Egypt. Cheetahs in Africa live in protected reserves and parks. It's especially important to protect the Cheetahs in Africa, because that's where the largest population remains.

Tan or light yellowish brown, black circles and spots

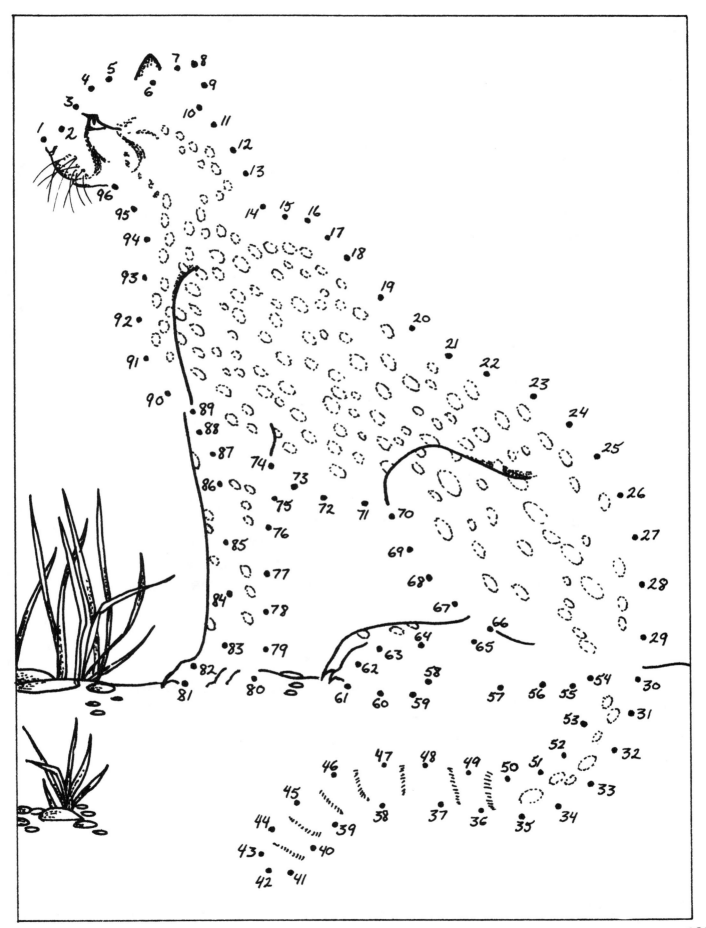

139

Name:	Desert Tortoise
Size:	Up to 14 inches (35cm) long
Where It Is Endangered:	Southwestern United States
Habitat:	Sandy and grassy desert areas

A Desert Tortoise is a very slow animal. It has strong feet and claws, and it digs burrows into the desert sand. It crawls into the burrows to get away from the sun and heat.

This reptile lives in the hot, dry desert of the American Southwest. There is very little rainfall, so the Desert Tortoise has to get its moisture from the plants it eats. The Desert Tortoise eats grasses, leaves and fruit. If no rain falls at all, there may be no green plants to eat, and the Tortoise may starve.

Brown, lighter yellowish brown patches on the shell. The cactus flowers are bright yellow.

Name:	Golden Toad
Size:	Almost 2 inches (5cm) long
Where It Is Endangered:	Costa Rica
Habitat:	Cloud forests and rain forests

All toads are amphibians—animals that can live in both land and water. Like other toads, Golden Toads eat insects.

Male Golden Toads are bright orange, but females are mostly green and black. Males gather together in groups to sing for mates, but only a few males have been found in the past few years. Once there were thousands, but now they are rare. The populations of toads from other parts of the world are decreasing also, so scientists are very concerned.

Bright orange-gold

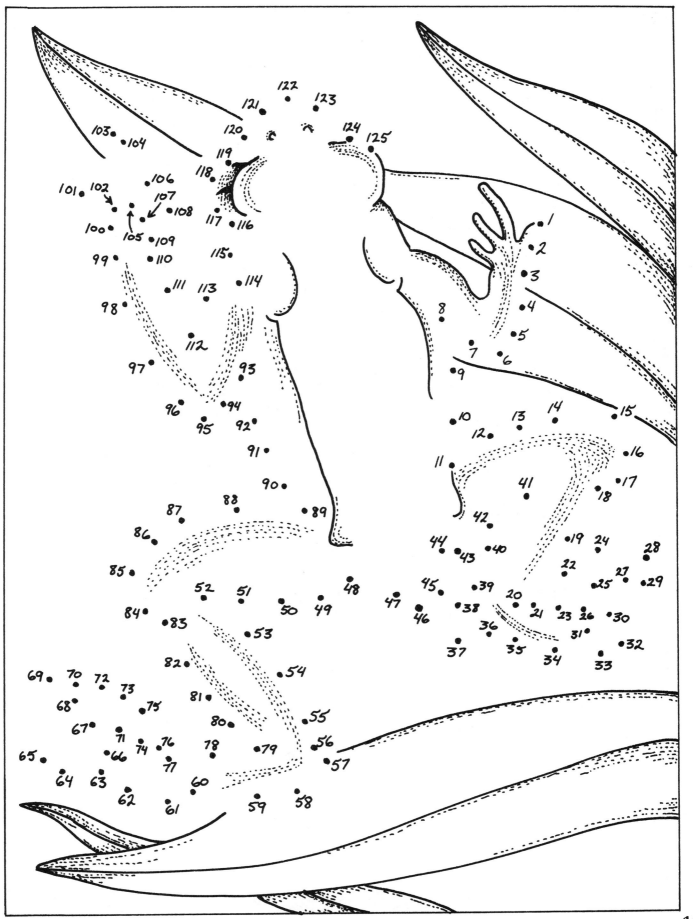

Name:	Gorgone Checkerspot
Size:	Wingspan: Less than 2 inches (5cm) across
Where It Is Endangered:	Illinois
Habitat:	Prairie fields and grassy meadows

This small butterfly is getting a great amount of attention! It has been found in many parts of the United States, but it is never very common. Conservationists are trying to start new populations in Illinois by bringing in Checkerspots from other areas.

All butterflies start out as caterpillars. The caterpillar of the Gorgone Checkerspot eats the leaves of asters and sunflowers.

The Gorgone Checkerspot is endangered because its home is often destroyed. When a field is mown or a road is built through a meadow, the habitat is ruined.

Orange and gold with black near the edge of the wing

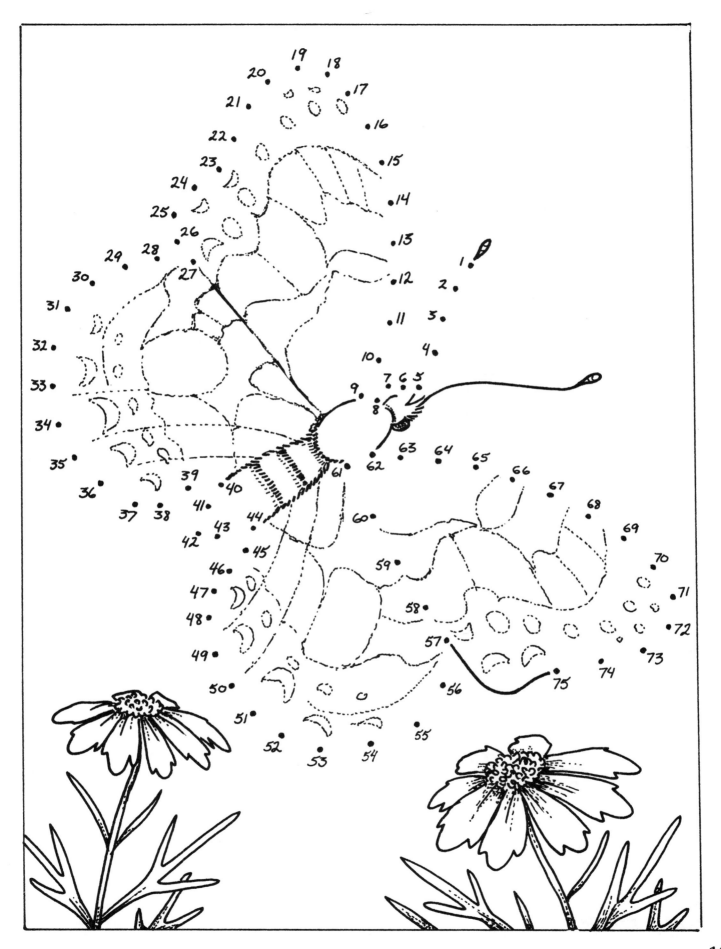

Name:	Kiwi
Size:	About 2 feet (.6m) long
Where It Is Endangered:	New Zealand
Habitat:	Pine forests with ferns

Kiwis are birds—but they can't fly. Their wings are much too small. All Kiwis have long thin beaks and strong legs. Their feathers are so thin and fine that they look like fur instead of feathers. Kiwis eat worms, insects and fruit, and are usually active at night.

Several different species of Kiwi live in New Zealand and Australia. In New Zealand, the Little Spotted Kiwi and the Brown Kiwi are protected. Protection is important: In one New Zealand sanctuary, more than a dozen Brown Kiwis were killed by just one dog!

This Kiwi is dark brown.

Name:	Koala
Size:	About 2 feet (.6m) tall
Where It Is Endangered:	Australia
Habitat:	Eucalyptus forests

This charming animal with hairy ears and a big nose is sometimes called a Koala Bear. But it isn't a bear at all, and it isn't even related to bears!

In Australia, the Koala is sometimes called the koolewong or the narnagoon, names given to it by the native Aborigines.

Koalas are great tree climbers. They eat only the leaves of eucalyptus trees. Zoos and wildlife parks that keep Koalas must have a steady supply of eucalyptus leaves to keep the Koalas healthy. There used to be millions of Koalas, but disease, hunting, and the cutting down of forests have decreased their population severely.

Golden brown or ash-brown fur, brownish black nose

Name:	Komodo Dragon
Size:	Up to 10 or 12 feet (3–3.6m) long
Where It Is Endangered:	Indonesia (Komodo Island and Rinca)
Habitat:	Island forests

The Komodo Dragon is the largest lizard in the world! Most Dragons live in a protected park on Komodo Island. They hunt for food during the day and spend nights in burrows in the ground. These huge reptiles kill and eat wild pigs and other small animals.

Protecting a rare animal like the Komodo Dragon can be difficult, because many people don't care about saving animals that are ugly or frightening. But wildlife workers at the Smithsonian's National Zoological Park have successfully hatched several young Dragons from eggs.

Black and brown. Young Komodo Dragons have lighter bands

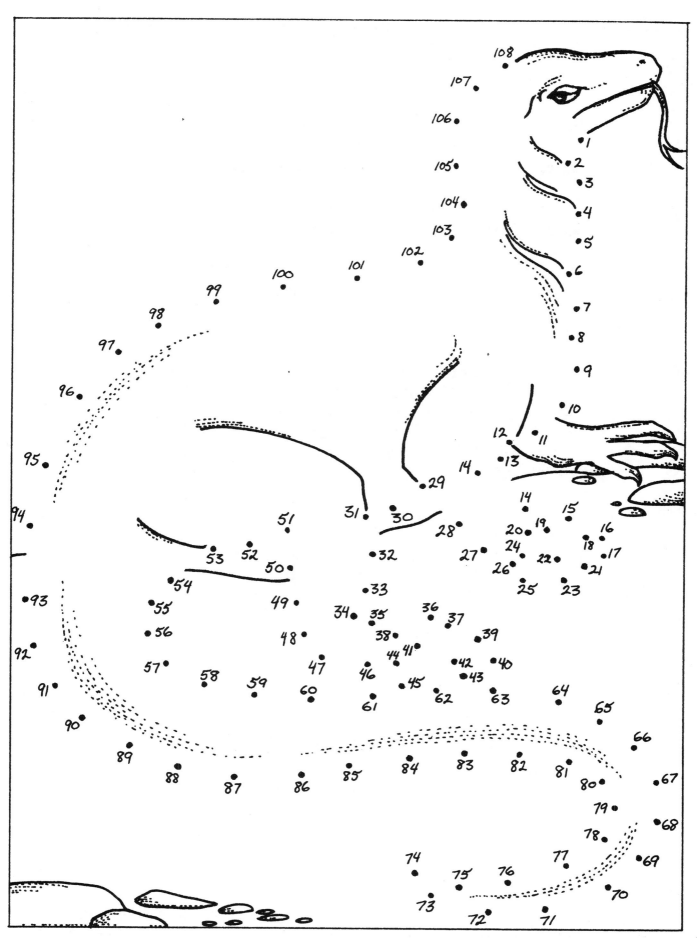

151

Name:	Panda
Size:	About 6 feet (1.8m) long
Where It Is Endangered:	Southwest China
Habitat:	Cold bamboo forests and mountains

Pandas are sometimes called Panda Bears, but they are not related to bears at all. The Panda's favorite foods include bamboo leaves and stems, fruit and berries. It also eats other plants and meat. A large full-grown Panda can eat as much as 40 pounds (18 kg) of bamboo in one day.

Many Pandas have been killed by hunters for their beautiful fur. Now people are very interested in protecting the Panda. Some zoos and wildlife parks have been successful in breeding Pandas, and some baby Pandas have been born in captivity. Conservationists hope this will keep the Panda from becoming extinct.

Snow-white head, black ears, a black spot around each eye, black legs and shoulders

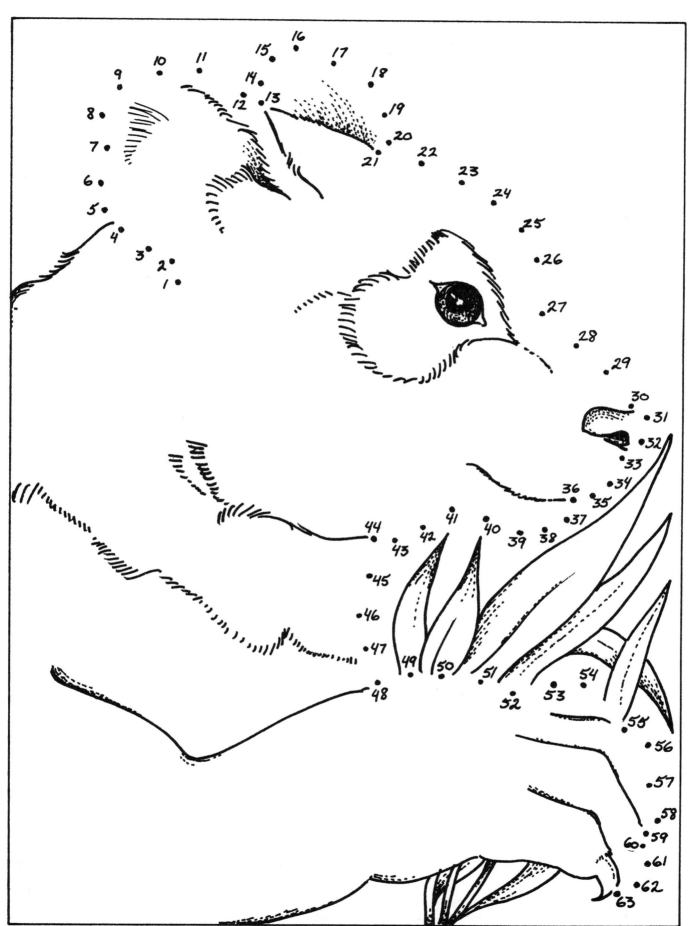

153

Name:	Snow Leopard
Size:	About 50 inches (125cm) long (not including the tail)
Where It Is Endangered:	Nepal (Central Asia)
Habitat:	. Remote mountains

The Snow Leopard is a hunter, like other members of the cat family. It tracks and eats wild sheep, hare, and even domestic livestock like goats. Snow Leopards hunt for food at dawn or at dusk.

These beautiful leopards have been killed for their fur, but now it is illegal to kill them.

Scientists have trapped some Snow Leopards and attached collars with radio transmitters to them. Tracking by radio helps the scientists learn where the cats travel and how big their territory is.

Pale yellow-tan (nearly white), black circles and spots

WILDLIFE
·················
DOT-TO-DOT

Monica Russo

Name:	Aardvark
Size:	5 to 6 feet (1.5–1.8m) long
Where it lives:	Southern Africa
What it eats:	Insects

The Aardvark is also called the Ant Bear, or the Earth Pig, but it is not related to either bears or pigs. It feeds during the night, hunting for ants and termites. The Aardvark uses its strong claws for digging and burrowing into the ground, searching for food. It has a long nose, and a long, sticky tongue for licking up ants from the ground.

An Aardvark may live to be about ten years old.

Reddish brown fur

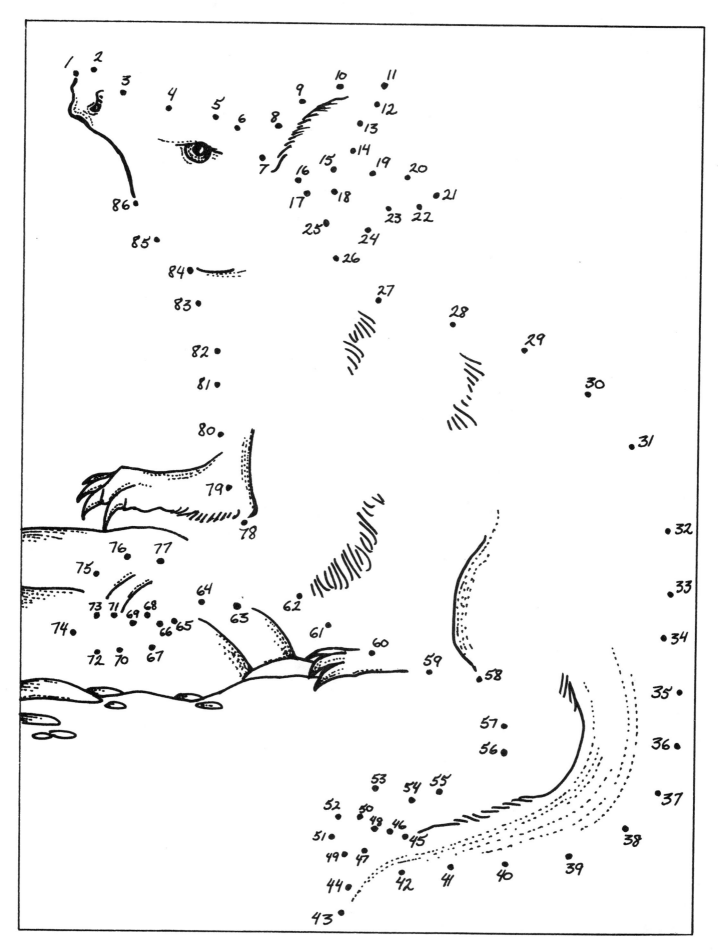

Name:	African Lion
Size:	About 8 feet (2.4m) long, with a 3-foot (.9m) tail
Where it lives:	Southern and central Africa
What it eats:	Other animals

African Lions are members of the cat family. They run very fast, reaching speeds of about 50 miles (80km) per hour for short distances. Lions hunt and eat wildebeests, impalas and even zebras, among other animals.

The male lion has a mane of long fur around its head and neck. Females don't have a mane and they are smaller than males. A group that lives and hunts together is called a "pride" of lions.

Sandy tan
The mane of the male is
dark brown.

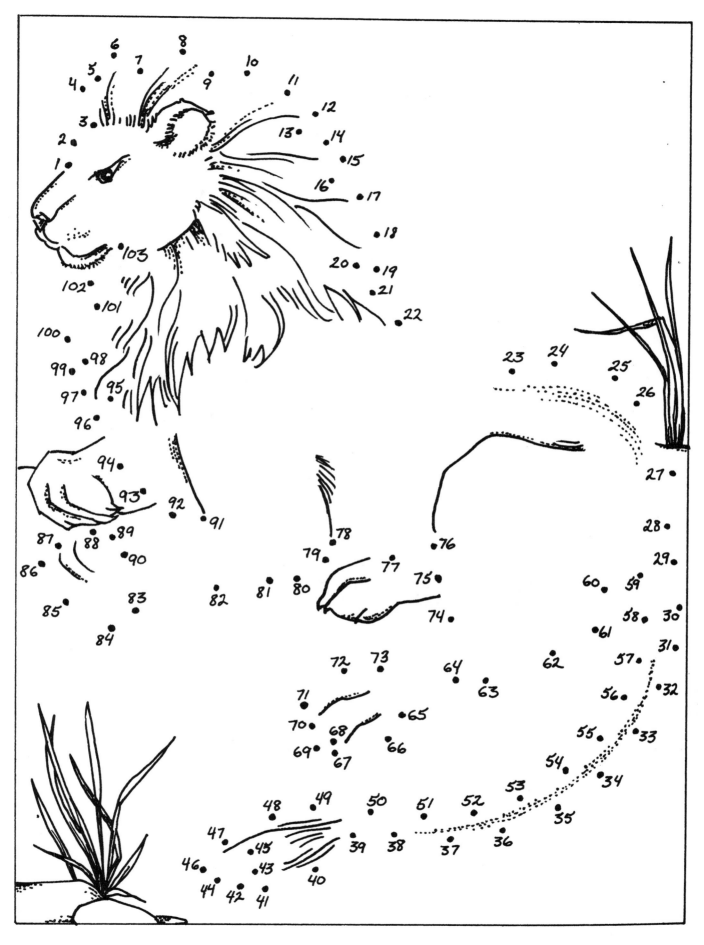

Name:	Badger
Size:	2 to 3 feet (.6—.09m) long
Where it lives:	U.K., Europe and Asia
What it eats:	Small animals, plants, and insects

The Badger is a member of the weasel family. It has strong claws on its front feet, which it uses to dig deep burrows when searching for food or building its den. The den of a Badger is called a "set" and it is underground. The Badger sleeps in its set during the daytime, but at night it hunts for mice, voles (small mouse-like rodents), snakes, birds, roots, acorns and beetles.

NOTE:
The Badger of North America is a different species. It is slightly smaller, but it looks and acts very much like the European Badger.

Head: wide black stripe from nose to ear
Body: grey or reddish-grey fur

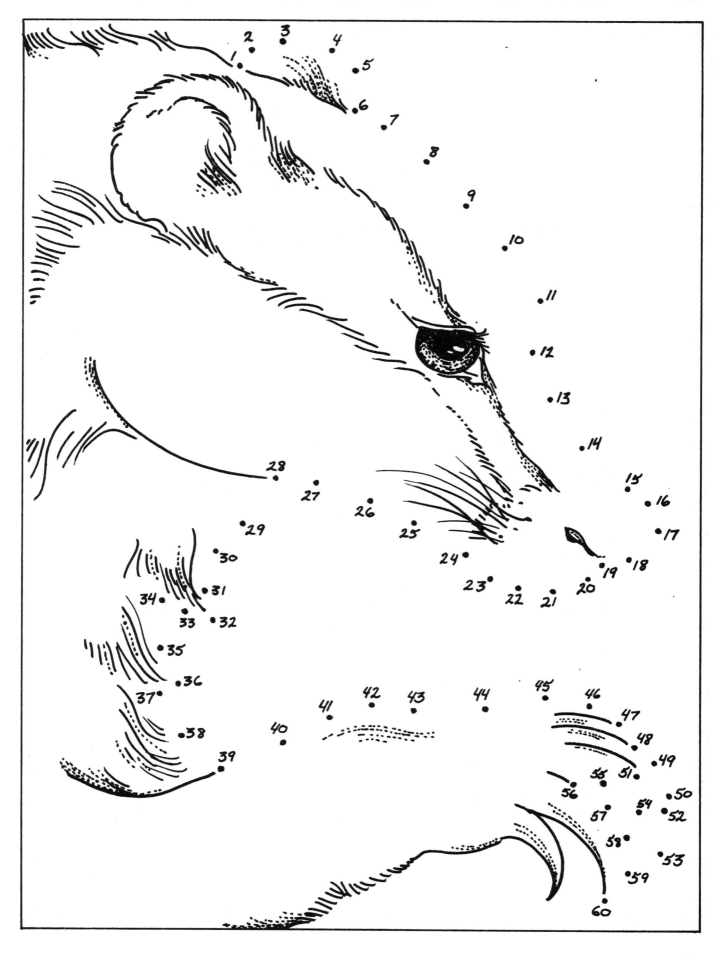

Name:	Barn Owl
Size:	About 14 to 20 inches (35–51cm) long
Where it lives:	North and South America, Africa, Asia, U.K., Australia
What it eats:	Mice and other small animals

There are more than 30 types of Barn Owls around the world. They all have a white, heart-shaped face, and light brown or buff bodies.

All Barn Owls are active at night, hunting mice, rats, voles, frogs, bats and insects. A Barn Owl can hear and see the slightest movements of a small mouse in the dark.

These ghostly owls don't hoot, but have a hoarse, raspy call instead. Most Barn Owls like to nest in the rafters of barns or abandoned buildings.

Face white, undersides white
Body: buff or sand colored

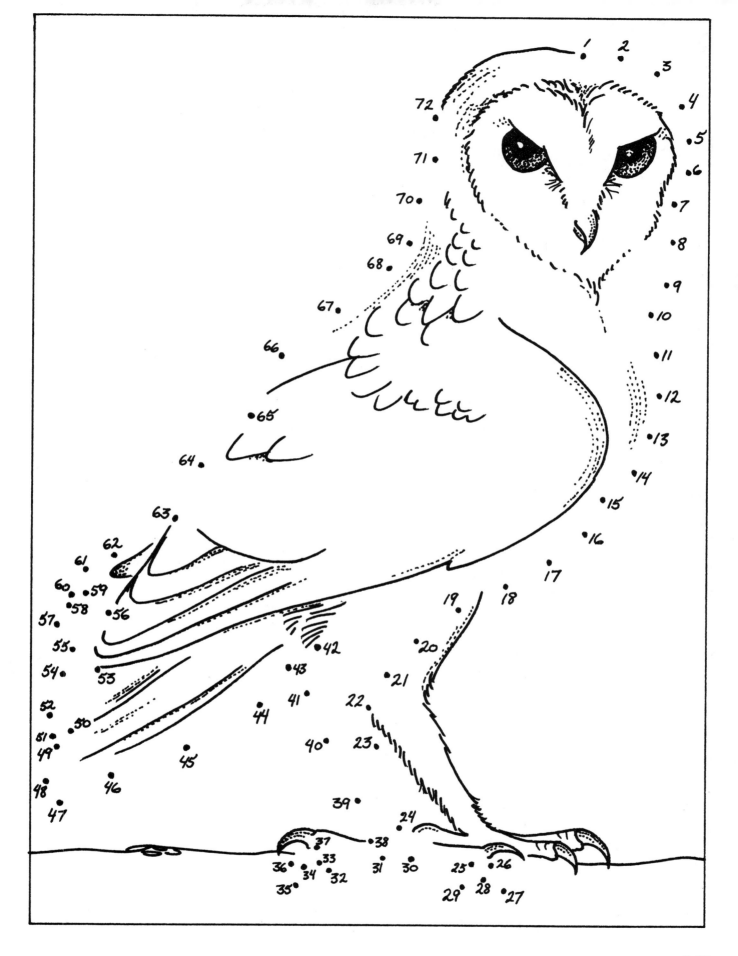

Name:	Black Rhinoceros
Size:	About 12 feet (3.6m) long
Where it lives:	Africa
What it eats:	Grasses, leaves and plant stems

The Black Rhino is an endangered species: there may be only about 2,000 left in Africa. Many rhinos have been killed by hunters for their valuable horns. Game wardens have started a program to saw off the horns of Black Rhinos, so that hunters won't shoot them. Some rhinos have been brought to zoos where their young can be born and raised in safety.

All rhinos have very thick, tough skin. They look hairless, but there are long hairs on their ears and the end of their tails.

Dark brownish grey

Name:	Bottle-nosed Dolphin
Size:	Up to 12 feet (3.6m) long
Where it lives:	Atlantic Ocean
What it eats:	Fish

This dolphin is named for its long narrow mouth. Bottle-nosed Dolphins are friendly, intelligent animals. They can make a variety of sounds—chirps, chatters, squeals and squeaks. Scientists have been working for many years to try to understand the language of dolphins.

Bottle-nosed Dolphins swim together in groups, or schools, hunting for fish. Young dolphins, called calves, may stay with their mothers for up to five years. Dolphins may live to be about 50 years old.

Dark grey along the top; light silvery grey or white underneath

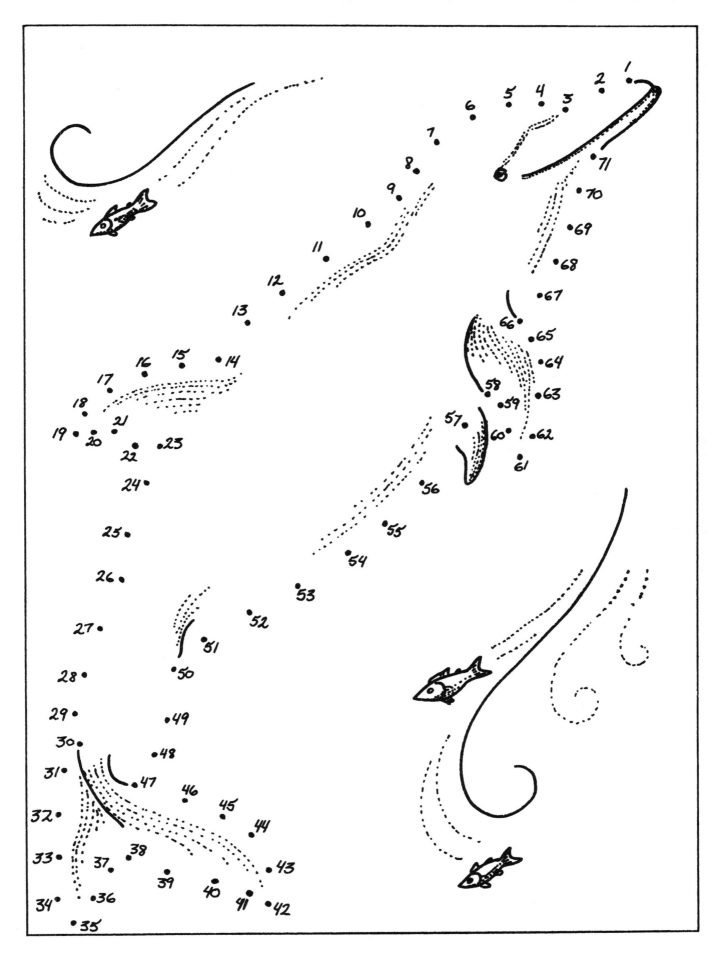

169

Name:	Emerald Tree Boa
Size:	Up to 12 feet (3.6m) long
Where it lives:	South America
What it eats:	Small animals

The Emerald Tree Boa is one of the most colorful snakes in the world. It is bright green—perfect camouflage for crawling around among jungle vines and branches! The Emerald Tree Boa hunts for birds, lizards and other small animals to eat. It coils tightly around its prey, crushing it to death.

Like other snakes, this Boa is a reptile. All reptiles have skin that is covered with small scales.

Bright green; white stripe down the back; yellowish lips; yellowish undersides

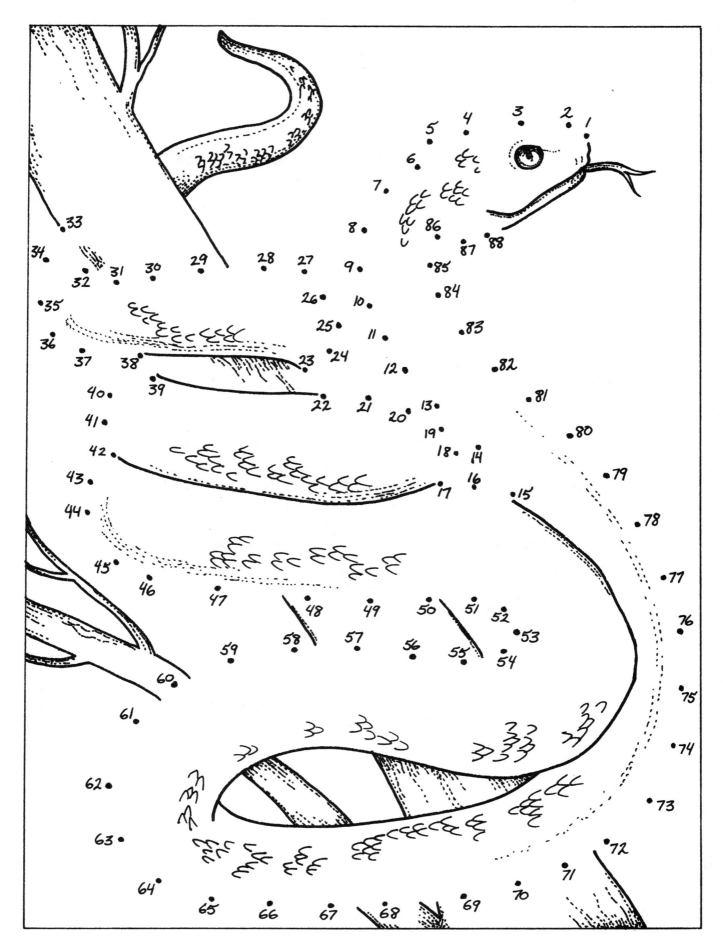

171

Name:	Giraffe
Size:	Its head is about 19 feet (5.8m) from the ground
Where it lives:	Africa
What it eats:	Plants

The Giraffe is well known for its graceful, long neck and long, thin legs. It can eat leaves, twigs and flowers from high branches.

At least two species of Giraffe live in Africa. Both have a pattern of dark brown blotches on their bodies. Giraffes have short, stubby horns on their heads and a short mane along the neck.

A running Giraffe can reach a speed of about 30 miles (48km) per hour, which is much slower than a galloping racehorse (that can go as fast as 40 miles/64km per hour).

Light tan, or yellowish white background, with dark brown blotches

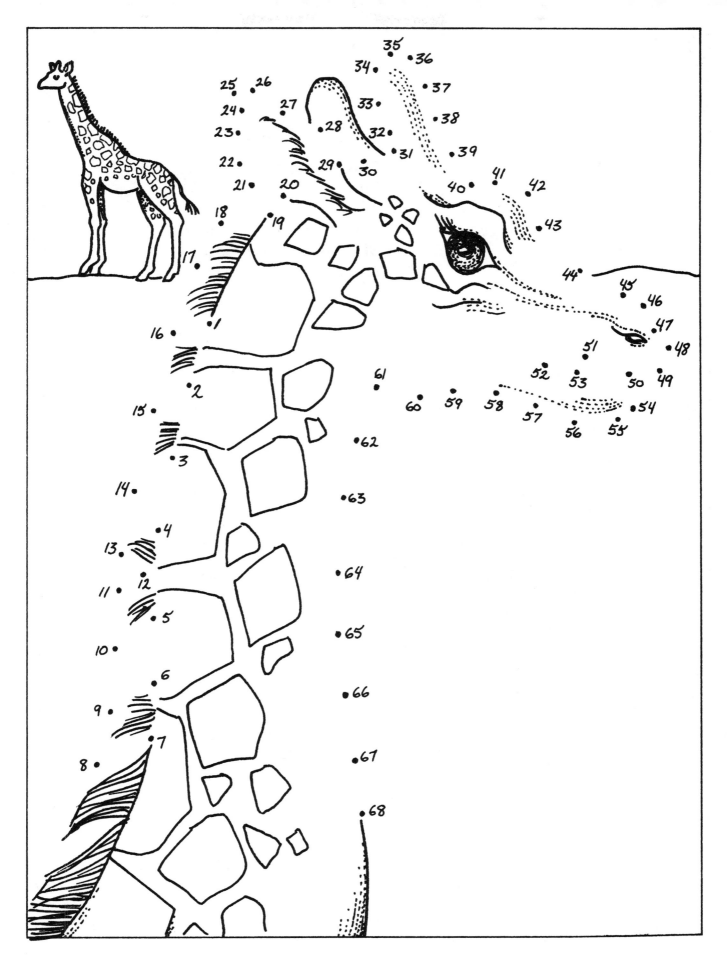

Name:	Green Sea Turtle
Size:	Shell is about 4 feet (1.2m) long
Where it lives:	Atlantic Ocean, Gulf of Mexico, Pacific Ocean, Mediterranean Sea
What it eats:	Sea plants

The Green Sea Turtle is a reptile, and has hard scales covering its head and legs. It spends most of its life in the ocean. It swims very well, because its front legs are shaped like flat flippers.

Female Sea Turtles leave the ocean only to lay eggs, crawling up on sandy shores. Some egg-laying sites are in Central America, the Philippines, and Malaysia. Green Sea Turtles were once caught and made into the once popular turtle soup, but now Sea Turtles in the Atlantic Ocean are protected by law.

Olive brown, with yellow bands or blotches

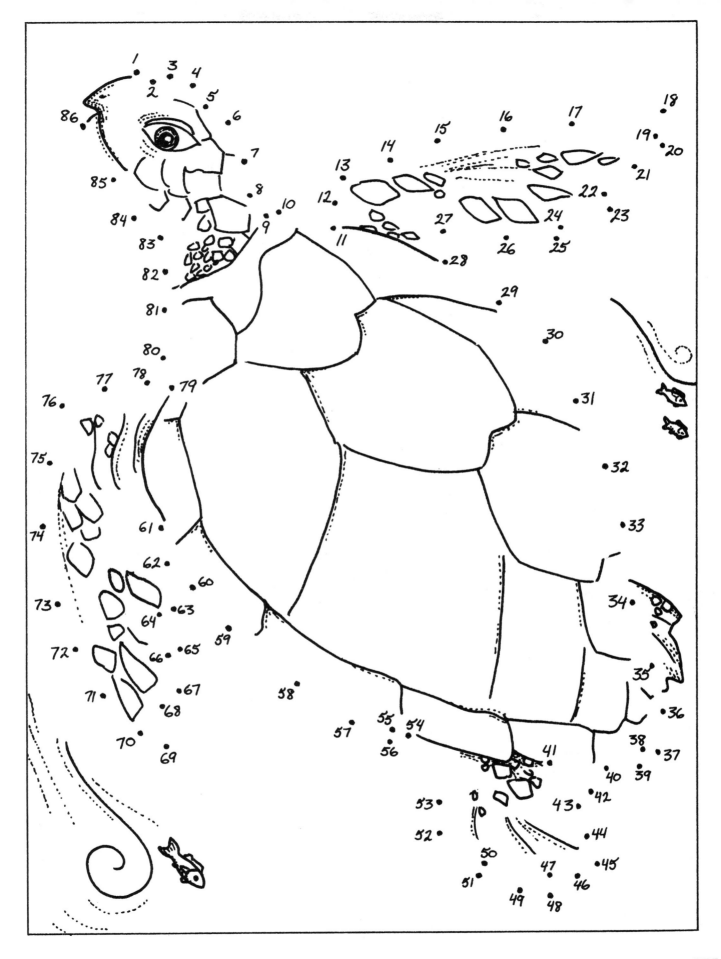

175

Name:	Hippopotamus
Size:	Up to 15 feet (4.6m) long
Where it lives:	Africa
What it eats:	Plants

Most people shorten the name Hippopotamus to "Hippo." Hippos have big, wide mouths, tough skin and very little hair!

Male Hippos (the larger ones) may weigh as much as four tons (3629kg). This huge mammal is a vegetarian, eating the roots and stems of underwater plants.

Hippos spend most of their time in rivers and lakes. They can float in the water, or sink down to eat plants. They can remain underwater for nearly 30 minutes. In the wild, they like to feed in groups or herds.

 Dark grey-brown

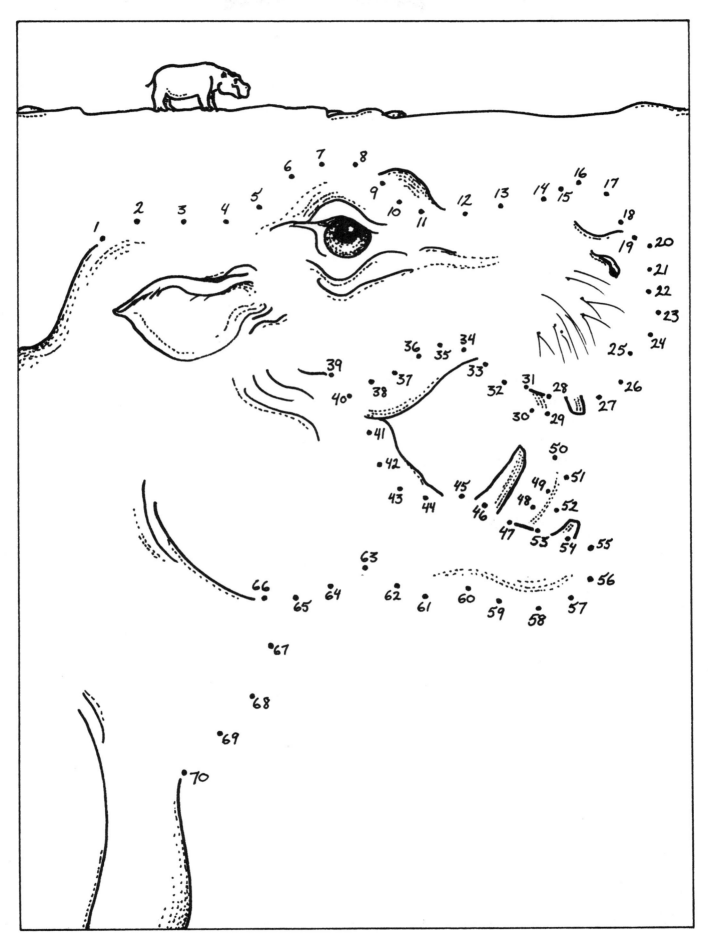

Name:	Indian Elephant
Size:	About 10 feet (3m) tall at the shoulder
Where it lives:	India and Asia
What it eats:	Plants

All elephants are vegetarian, eating leaves, grasses and twigs. There are two kinds of elephants, Indian and African. The Indian Elephant is a little smaller than the African—it can weigh as much as six tons (5443kg). Most Indian Elephants have long tusks, but not all.

If you want to tell Indian and African elephants apart when you see them at the circus or on TV, look at their ears! Indian Elephants have much smaller ears than African Elephants. They are also easier to tame and train. They have been used as working animals, moving large logs and other heavy objects. African elephants are rarely used as workers.

Dark grey-brown

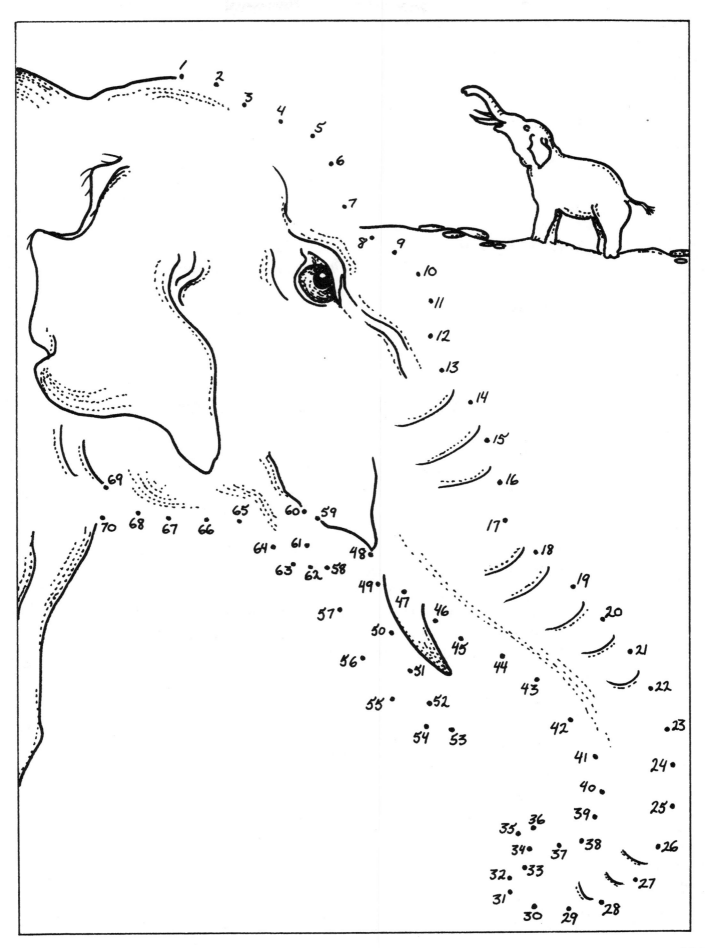

Name:	Mongoose
Size:	About 18 to 30 inches (45–76cm) long, not including the tail
Where it lives:	Africa, India, China, Borneo, Malaya, Java
What it eats:	Small animals

The Mongoose looks like a weasel but is not related to it. It is a very quick animal, and can jump, charge, leap and twist with speed. Because it is so fast and agile, the Mongoose is famous for being able to kill poisonous snakes, like the deadly Indian cobra.

There are several types of Mongoose around the world—but none are found in the wild in North or South America. Some were brought to Hawaii, and they nearly killed off all the ground-nesting birds! A Mongoose will eat all types of small animals: insects, birds, mice, rats, and even frogs.

 Grey-brown

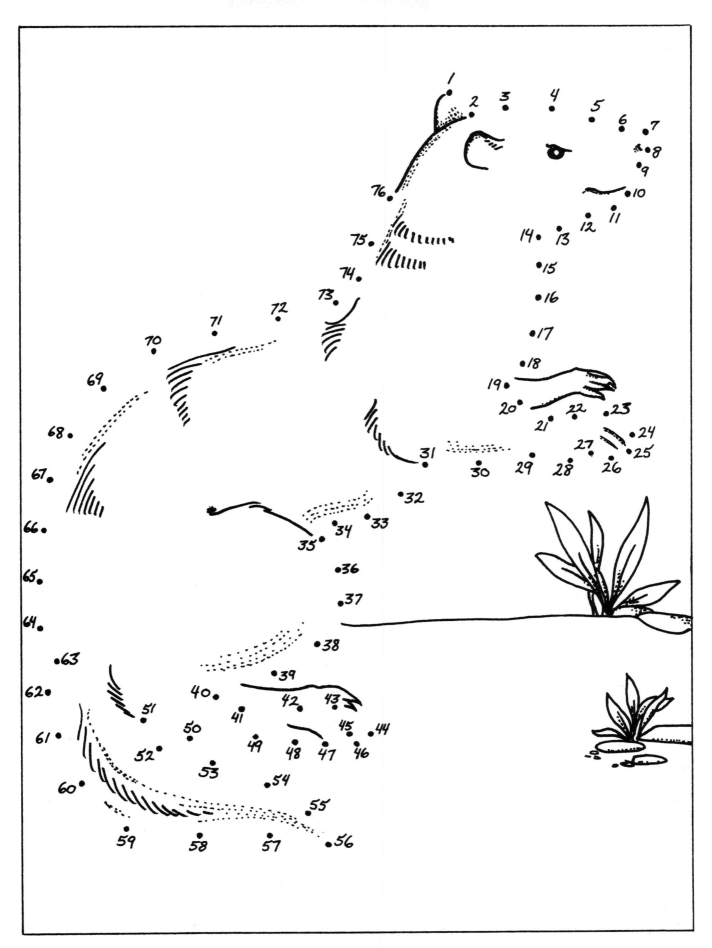

Name:	Mute Swan
Size:	About 5 feet (1.5m), from beak to tail
Where it lives:	Europe, U.K., Asia
What it eats:	Water plants and seeds

This large white waterbird is a graceful swimmer and powerful in flight. While its natural habitat is in Europe and Asia, it is often raised in other parts of the world, as well.

When swimming on lakes and ponds, the Mute Swan holds its neck in a curve. Other types of swans swim with straight necks. When disturbed by other animals or by people, Mute Swans will hiss, snort and grunt loudly.

Male swans are called "cobs." Young swans, called "cygnets," are light brown.

Snowy white, with a bright orange beak

Name:	Platypus
Size:	Up to 2 feet (61cm) long
Where it lives:	Australia and Tasmania
What it eats:	Insects, worms and tadpoles

The Platypus is such a strange animal that—when skins were first brought to Europe—people thought it was fake! It has a flat, rubbery mouth that looks like a duck's bill—no other fur-bearing animal on earth has that!

The Platypus lives in freshwater streams and lakes, using its webbed feet like paddles to swim underwater. The female uses her strong claws to dig burrows in the ground above the waterline, and make a nest of leaves and grass. She then lays *eggs* in the nest, instead of giving birth to live babies, like other furry animals do!

The fine, velvety fur of the Platypus is dark brown-grey.

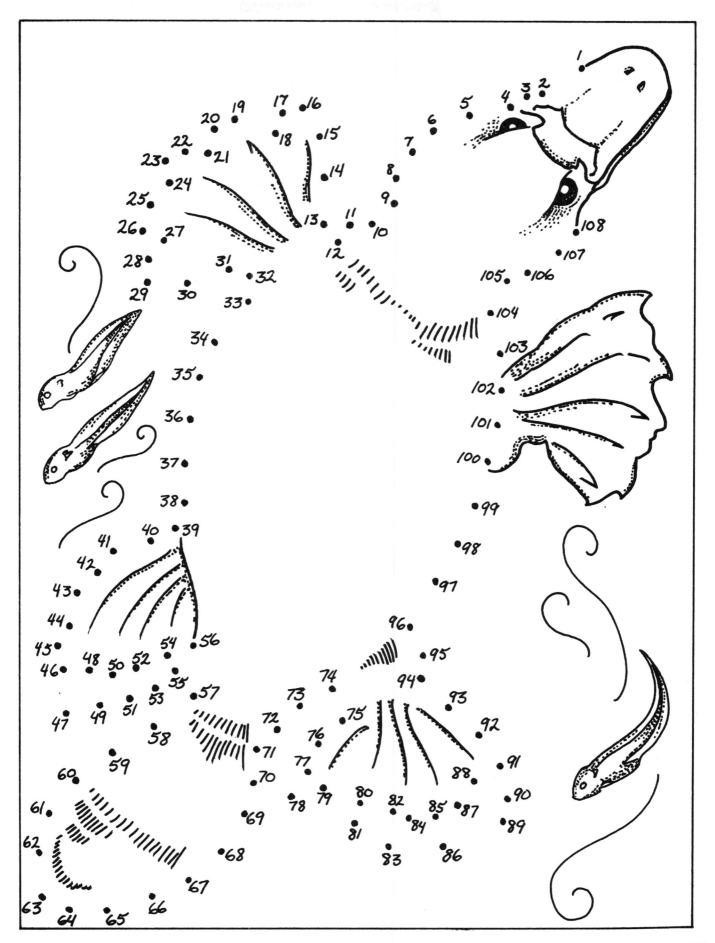

Name:	Polar Bear
Size:	About 5 feet (1.5m) high at the shoulder
Where it lives:	Arctic tundra of northern Canada, Russia and Greenland
What it eats:	Other animals and some plants

The Polar Bear is one of the largest meat-eating land animals. When it stands on its hind legs, it's about ten feet (3m) tall! This huge mammal hunts seals mostly, but also eats lemmings and ducks.

Polar Bears live in a habitat of snow and ice all year, so they have a thick fur coat. They even have fur on the soles of their feet!

Polar Bears do *not* live at the South Pole. They don't live near penguins at all, even though cartoons sometimes show Polar Bears and penguins in the snow together.

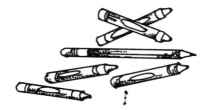 White to yellowish white

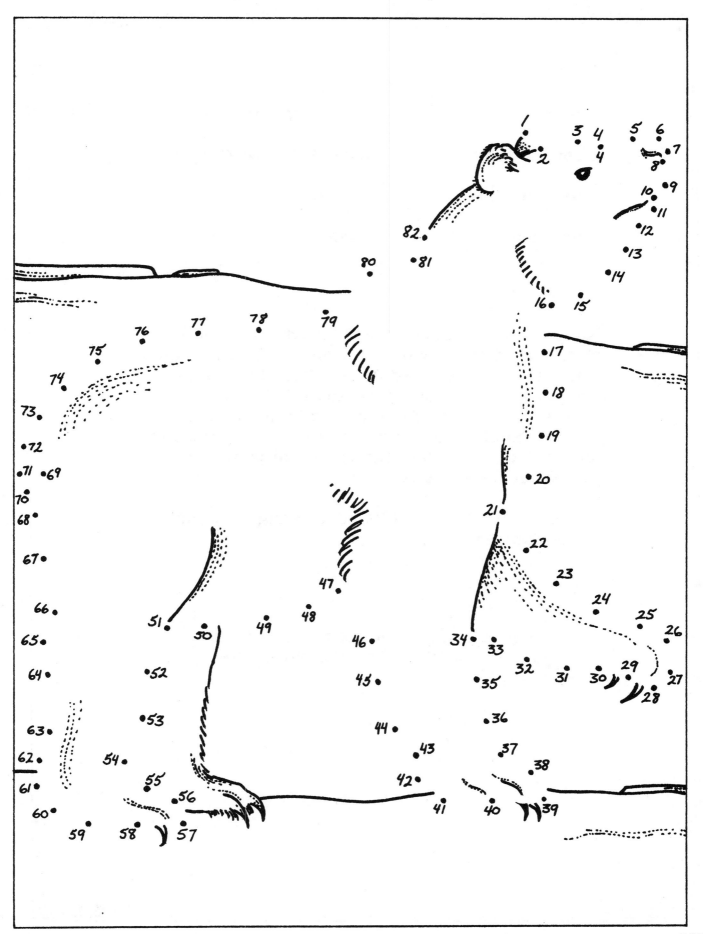

187

Name:	Red Kangaroo
Size:	About 9 feet (2.7m) long
Where it lives:	Australia
What it eats:	Plants

Kangaroos are known for their long tails and strong hind legs. With one leap, the Red Kangaroo can cover a distance of 30 feet (91m)! The Red Kangaroo is the largest of Australia's "roos." It eats grasses and leaves, feeding mostly at night. A young roo is called "Joey." A Joey spends the first few months of its life inside a large pouch or pocket on the female's belly.

Wallabies, which look like small kangaroos, are close relatives.

Male: rusty red
Female: bluish grey

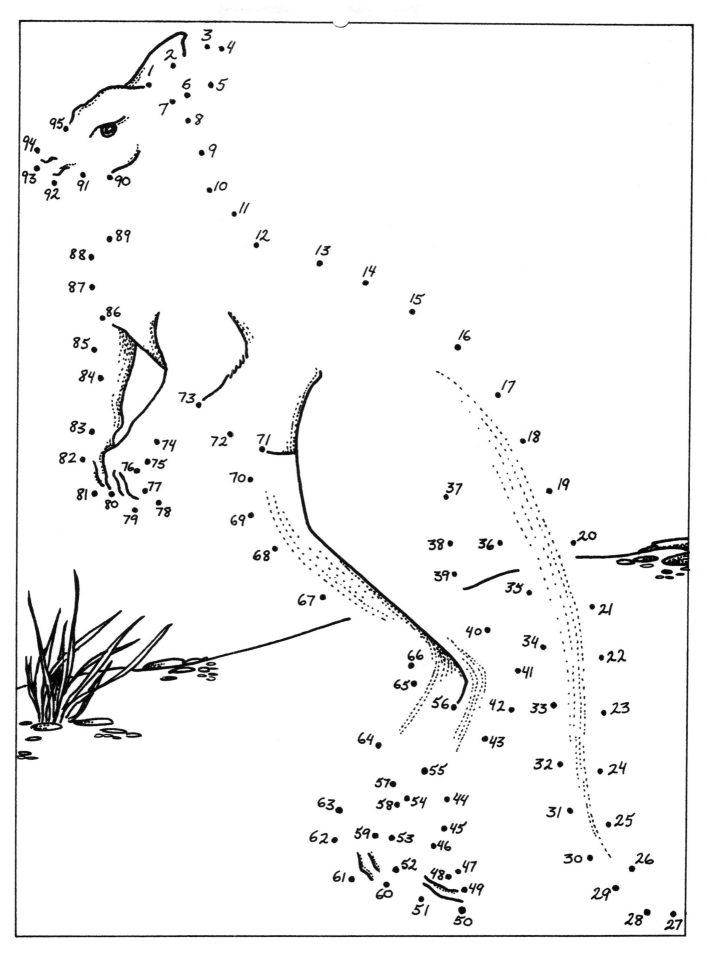

Name:	Siberian Tiger
Size:	About 13 feet (4m) long
Where it lives:	Russia, China and North Korea
What it eats:	Animals

The Siberian Tiger is a member of the cat family. Its relatives include jaguars, leopards, lions, bobcats and ocelots. There are several other kinds of tigers: the Bengal Tiger of India, the Sumatran Tiger, Bali Tiger, and Javan Tiger, to name a few. The Siberian Tiger is the largest. All tigers hunt and kill other animals. The Siberian Tiger is rare, and is protected by laws against hunters. Scientists are hoping to breed and raise these endangered animals.

Very light tan, with grey-brown stripes

191

Name:	Spotted Salamander
Size:	About 7 inches (17cm) long
Where it lives:	Canada and the U.S.
What it eats:	Insects and worms

This amphibian is named for the bright yellow or orange dots on its dark skin. Like other amphibians, it is active on land and in water, and is an excellent swimmer.

It lays its eggs in ponds, and the young salamanders grow up in the water. Adult Spotted Salamanders are found in springs, swamps and wet woods as well as in ponds.

Many different types of salamanders (and their close relatives, the newts) are found nearly worldwide. The Spotted Salamander of Europe, though, is a different species from the one in North America. It is sometimes called the Fire Salamander.

Dark grey or black background
Bright orange or yellow spots

Name:	Walkingstick
Size:	About 2 to 12 inches (5—30cm) long
Where it lives:	North America to South America; Australia, Asia and Africa
What it eats:	Plants

Walkingsticks look like moving, walking twigs! These strange insects have a long, skinny body and thin twiggy legs. Most Walkingsticks are green or brown. Because of their shape and coloring, they are well camouflaged on branches, and hard to find. They eat the leaves of trees and shrubs. Most Walkingsticks are only a few inches long, but one species from Borneo is about a foot (30cm) long!

 Green and brown

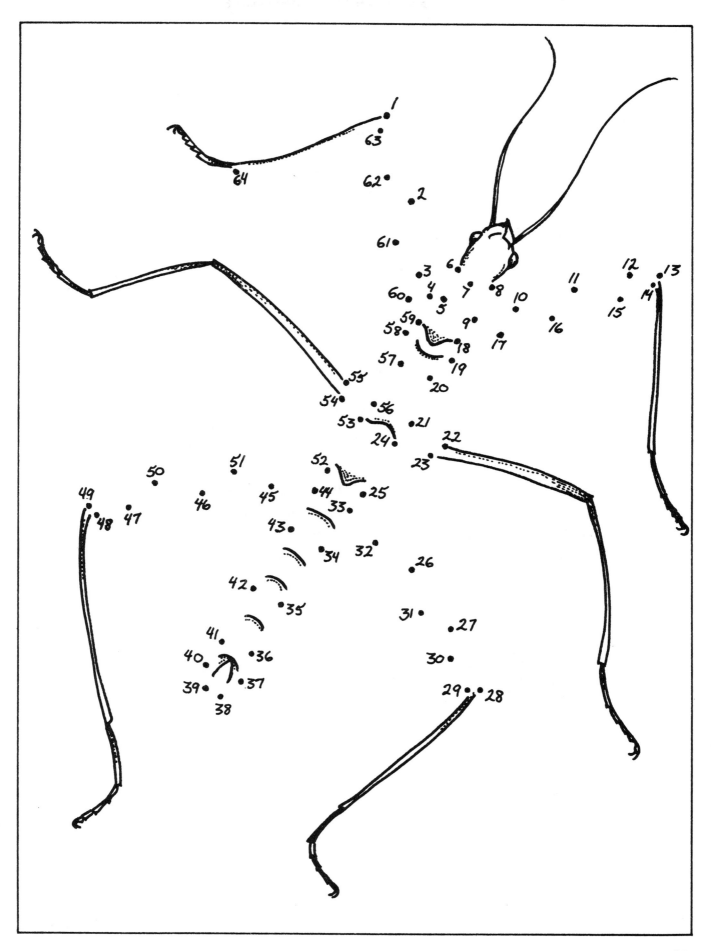

Name:	Zebra
Size:	Up to 58 inches (147cm) at the shoulder
Where it lives:	Africa
What it eats:	Plants

Zebras are native to Africa, and there are several types. They all look like small horses with stripes. Some types of Zebra have very narrow stripes, and some have no stripes at all on the belly. All have short manes.

Zebras can run about 40 miles (64km) per hour. Birds called Oxpeckers sometimes ride on the backs of Zebras, eating off insects and ticks from the Zebra's fur. This gives the Oxpecker food and it keeps the Zebra comfortable.

White, with black stripes

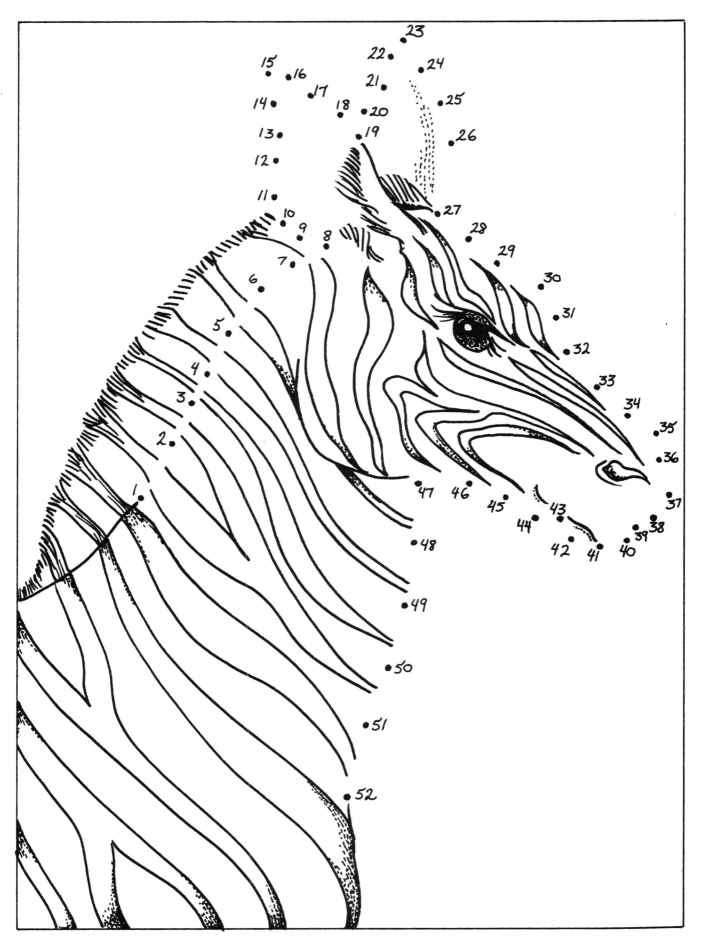

Mythical Animals Dot-to-Dot

Monica Russo

Name:	BASILISK
How to say it:	BASS ih lisk
Other name:	King of Serpents, because it has the pattern of a crown on its head
Where it lives:	In hot, dry places in Europe, the Mideast and Asia
Where the myth or legend started:	Roman legend

Legend

The Basilisk is small, but very powerful. It can kill animals with just one glance from its bright yellow eyes. Its poisonous breath can wilt plants. Even its hiss could kill a person!

The Basilisk comes from the egg of a rooster, hatched by a toad or snake.

The only way a Basilisk can be killed is to see itself in a mirror.

Only one animal is safe from
the Basilisk's stare—the weasel!

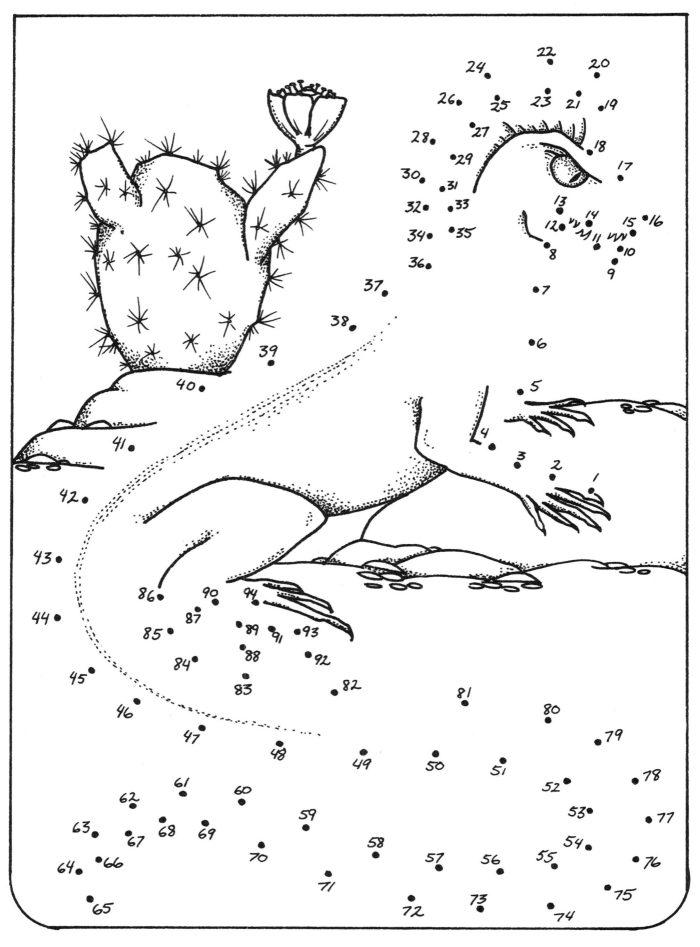

Name:	BUTO
How to say it:	BU to
Other name:	Vazit
Where it lives:	Egypt
Coloring tip:	Use red, blue and gold.
Where the myth or legend started:	Egyptian mythology

Legend

Buto is a goddess of the ancient Egyptian kings. She is part cobra, and part vulture, with beautiful wide wings. Endowed with great power, Buto protected people from their enemies.

The Egyptian King Tutankhamen wore a gold headband with Buto on the front of it.

Buto sometimes has a crown
on her head: it's the red disk
of the sun.

Name:	CHIMERA
How to say it:	kih MEER ah (Many people call it SHI-murra.)
Where it lived:	Greece and Rome
Where the myth or legend started:	Greek mythology

Legend

The Chimera was one of the most frightening monsters ever imagined. It was *very* dangerous. It had the head and body of a lion, and a second head that looked like a goat or ram. The tail of the Chimera was a long, deadly snake.

A brave warrior named Bellerophon was sent out to find the Chimera, and kill it. Riding on the wonderful flying horse, Pegasus, Bellerophon was able to kill this horrible monster.

The Chimera breathed fire.

Name: CHINESE DRAGON

Where it lives: China

Coloring tip: *Warning:* Finishing a picture of a Chinese dragon can cause a bad storm, especially if the dragon isn't happy with your picture!

Where the myth or legend started: Chinese legends

Legend

Chinese dragons can bring good luck—if you can find one! They can change their shape, turn into a tiny silkworm, or even hide behind a rainbow. They can travel anywhere they want to—up into the clouds—or deep down into a well. Chinese dragons can be frightened away by anything made of iron, and by centipedes.

Dragons can breathe smoke and fire.

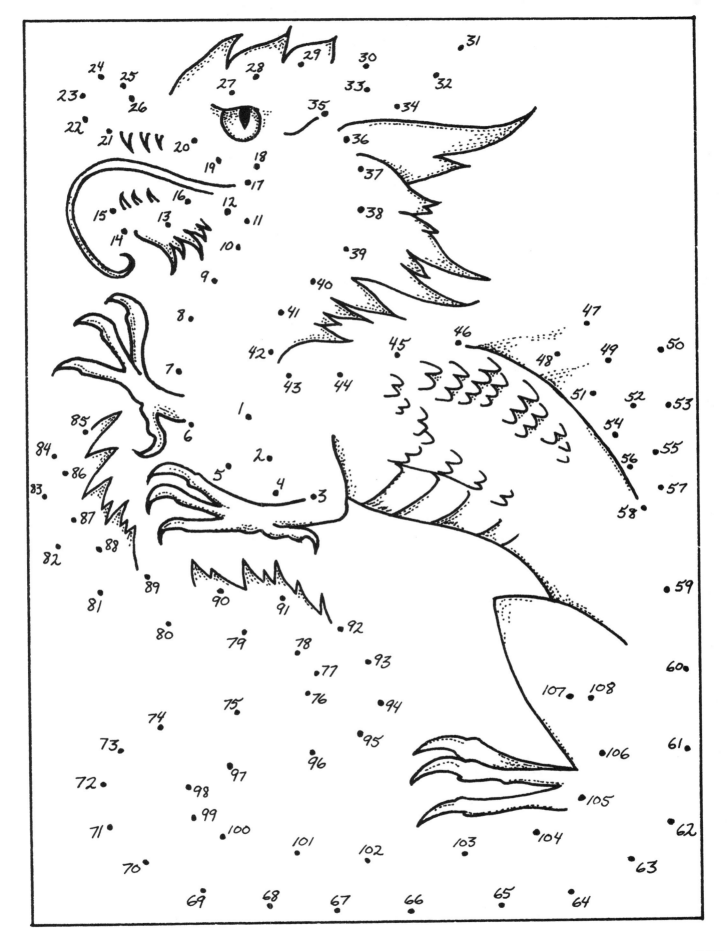

Name:	CRIOSPHINX
How to say it:	CRY oh sfinks **or:** CREE oh sfinks
Where it lives:	Egypt
Coloring tip:	The headdress of this Sphinx is colored red, blue and gold.
Where the myth or legend started:	Egyptian mythology

Legend

Every Sphinx is a guardian. It protects tombs and secret places; and it guards pathways.

A Sphinx always has the body of a lion. Sometimes it has the head of a woman, but the Criosphinx has the head of a ram. Rams were sacred to the Egyptians. A row of Criosphinxes line each side of the road that leads to a temple in Egypt. The statues were built thousands of years ago, and are still there, guarding the temple.

There are several different ram-headed creatures. This one's name is Khnum, and he was one of the gods of the Nile.

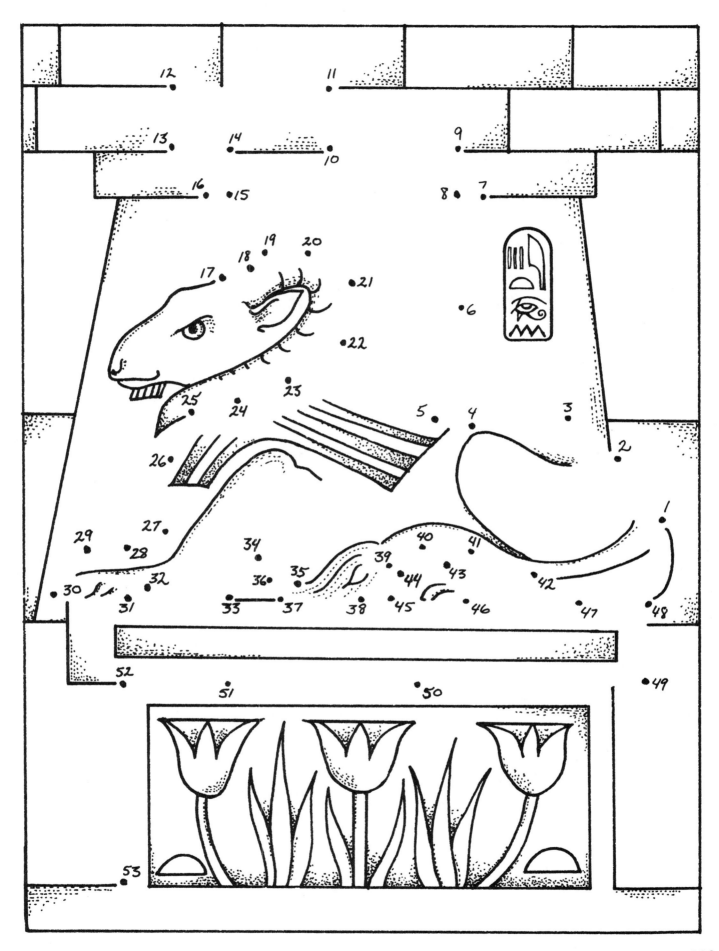

Name:	DRACO
How to say it:	DRAY ko
Other names:	Old Serpent
Where it lives:	In the sky, with the stars
Where the myth or legend started:	Greek mythology

Legend

During the spring and summer, you can see a pattern of stars that looks like a long snake, or dragon—that's Draco. It has a star for each eye.

Draco is a Greek name, meaning dragon.

The tail of Draco lies between the Big Dipper and the Little Dipper.

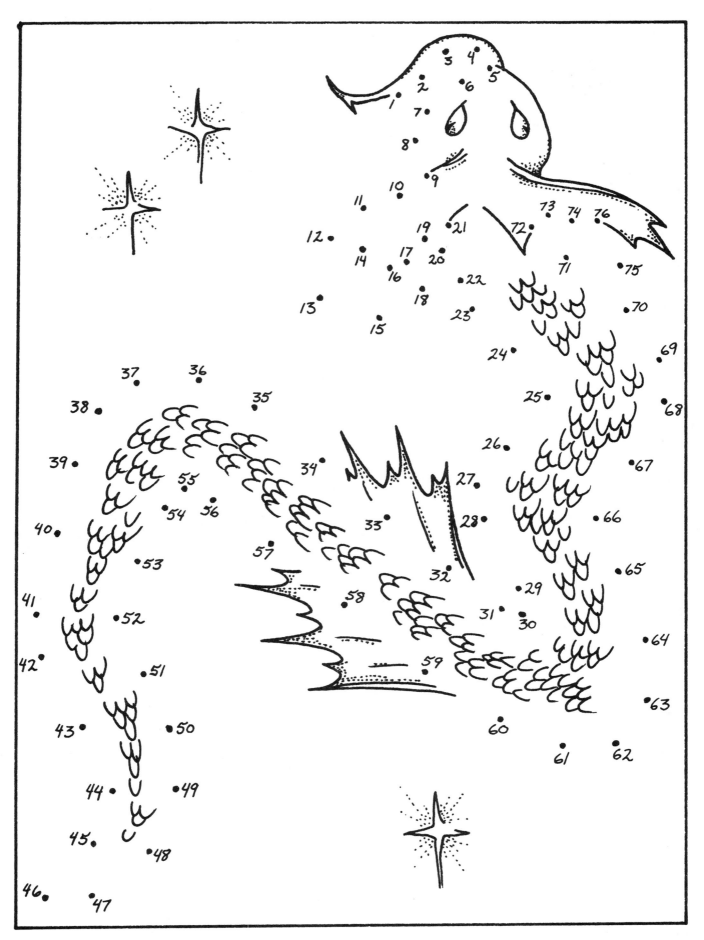

211

Name:	EAGLE SPIRIT
How to say it:	Some Native American words for "Eagle" are: Kupitalik (Ku PEET alik), Mutughowik (Mu TUG oh wik), Tiggalach (TIG ah lak).
Where it lives:	United States and Canada
Coloring tip:	Use red, black and apple green.
Where the myth or legend started:	North America, in Native American legends

Legend

Eagles are real birds, of course. The spirit of the eagle is powerful, so Native Americans admired these birds very much.

Tribes in the Northwest painted and carved the Eagle Spirit on wood. They also carved eagles on tall totem poles.

Eagle Spirits and other birds were painted on blankets and capes, too.

213

Name:	GRIFFIN
How to say it:	GRIF in
Where it lives:	India, Russia and China
Where the myth or legend started:	Greek, Roman and Scythian legends

Legend

Griffins have the heads of eagles, but their other parts can vary. Some have eagle wings, and some have bat wings. Some Griffins have horns, and some have both fur and feathers.

Griffins live high in the mountains, where they guard their nests fiercely. Their nests are lined with pure gold!

Some Griffins are dangerous and breathe fire. Others are very friendly.

All Griffins have wings, but some are not able to fly well.

215

Name:	HORUS
How to say it:	HOH russ
Where it lives:	In the heavens
Where the myth or legend started:	Egyptian mythology

Legend

Horus is the Egyptian sun god. He is part human and part falcon, and he is shown with an orange sun above his head. Horus brings the sun across the sky each day. He is always fighting against darkness.

Thousands of years ago, good-luck charms called amulets were carved in the shape of the falcon Horus. Some of them were made out of gold. These charms were meant to bring safety, health and strength to their owners.

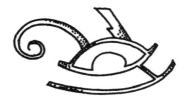

This is the Eye of Horus—
a design the Egyptians used
in making jewelry thousands
of years ago.

Name:	HYDRA
How to say it:	HY dra
Where it lived:	In a lake or swamp in Greece
Coloring tip:	The middle head was the color of bright gold.
Where the myth or legend started:	Greek mythology

Legend

Hydra was a cruel water monster with nine heads. Whenever one was cut off, a new one grew in its place. The middle head was the largest, and it was immortal. The Hydra was so poisonous that its breath—or touch—caused death.

The Greek hero Hercules was the only person able to kill the Hydra. He cut off all the heads, burned the necks (so a new head wouldn't grow back) and then buried the middle head under a rock. This was one of the greatest feats Hercules ever performed.

The Hydra had a long tail but no hind feet.

Name:	JAPANESE DRAGON
Where it lives:	Japan
Coloring tip:	Japanese dragons are very colorful—you can use red, blue, green and gold.
Where the myth or legend started:	Japan

Legend

Dragons are very powerful. At one time, it was believed that clouds were really dragon breath. Dragon breath was so strong that it could create hurricanes, storms and tornadoes.

Some dragons were also said to be rich. They liked to collect pearls, gems and beautiful stones.

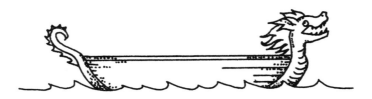

Some Japanese boats were made with a dragon-shaped head and tail.

221

Name:	KRAKEN
How to say it:	KRAY ken
Where it lives:	In the ocean
Where the myth or legend started:	Norse mythology

Legend

You'll never see a whole Kraken all at once. It's so big, you can only see a part of it at a time!

The Kraken is a sea monster that causes powerful whirlpools in the oceans. The swirling pools trap ships, and cause shipwrecks. The only time it is safe to see a Kraken is on a hot, sunny, summer day when the sea is calm.

The Kraken has long tentacles and big horns.

223

Name:	LEVIATHAN
How to say it:	leh VY ah thin
Where it lives:	In the ocean
Where the myth or legend started:	Biblical legend

Legend

Leviathan is so huge that it can encircle the whole earth! Its body is so long it takes up all the oceans in the world.

This very big and very powerful sea monster is the largest creature ever imagined. Leviathan eats smaller sea serpents. It has such bright eyes, they light up the water all around it, even in the deepest, darkest oceans.

Leviathan is so big that sea serpents
look small next to it.

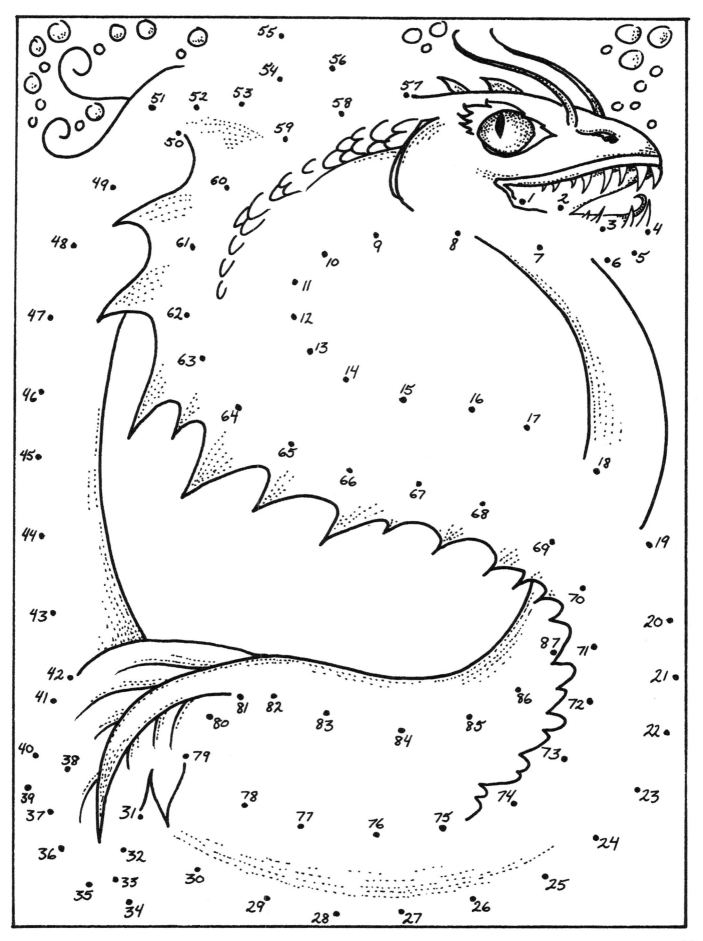

225

Name:	LOCH NESS MONSTER
How to say it:	lahk ness
Other name:	Some people call the Loch Ness Monster "Nessie."
Where it lives:	In a lake in northern Scotland
Where the myth or legend started:	Scottish legend

Legend

In Scotland, a lake is called a loch. In the deep waters of Loch Ness, this mysterious creature is said to be hiding. Many people say they have seen it, and claim that photos have shown a part of it. But when people try to get a close-up look at the Loch Ness Monster, they can't. It dives deep underwater, they say. The lake is over 900 feet deep!

No one knows for sure if Nessie is
a sea serpent, a huge reptile,
some kind of dinosaur, or just imaginary.

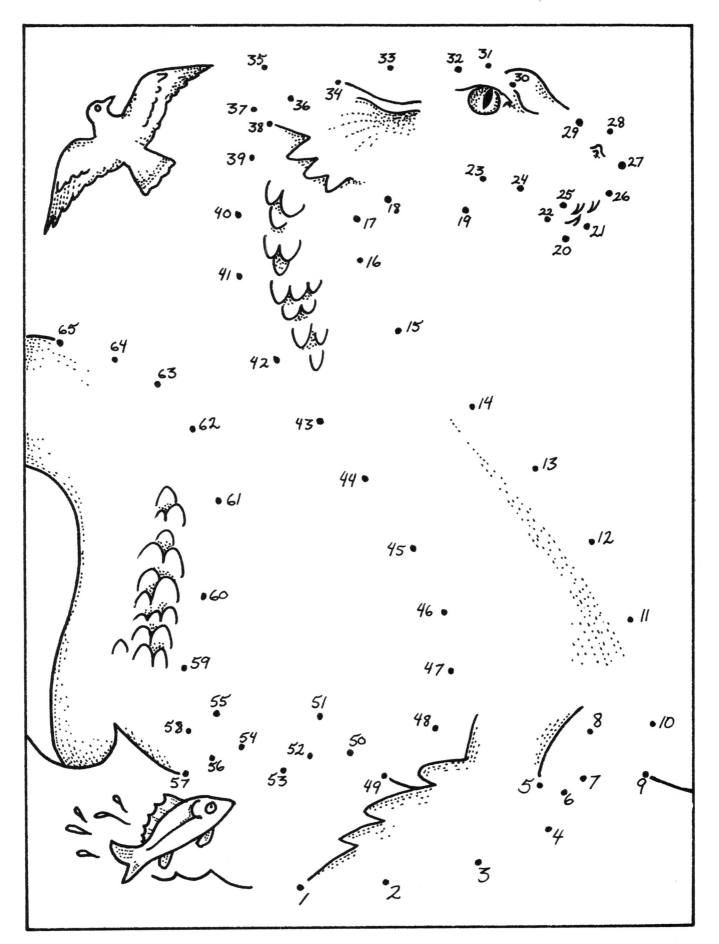

Name:	MAYA EARTH MONSTER
How to say it:	MY ah
Where it lives:	Central America
Where the myth or legend started:	Central America and the northern part of South America

Legend

This monster looks something like a large reptile—maybe a crocodile or an iguana. It has huge claws, and long feathers for its tail.

The Mayan Indians held ceremonies where important people dressed up in costumes like huge reptiles. All animals were important to the Mayan Indians, and some were thought to have magical powers.

These are some of the trees
that grew near the Earth Monster's home.

Name:	MAYA SKY SERPENT
How to say it:	MY ah
Where it lives:	Central America
Coloring tip:	Color your Sky Serpent with the same colors the Mayans used: red, green, black and yellow.
Where the myth or legend started:	Central America and northern South America

Legend

The Sky Serpent is a rain god, a very helpful god that helps to make the corn grow. The sound of thunder is really the strong voice of the Maya Sky Serpent.

The Mayans painted pictures of the Sky Serpent on tree bark hundreds of years ago. This god-creature wears a fancy crest on its head.

This is the Maya symbol for the fifth day of the month—it has part of the Sky Serpent's skin pattern on it.

Name:	NIDHUGG
How to say it:	NEED hoog
Where it lives:	In a dark place at the bottom of the world
Where the myth or legend started:	Norse mythology

Legend

The Nidhugg is a Norwegian water monster that lives in a dark, evil land of ice and snow.

To get to the Nidhugg's den, you must travel for nine days through dark forests, deep valleys and frightening caves. Nidhugg lives underwater, guarding a spring. The only words he speaks are insults, threats and nasty remarks. These ugly words are carried to the rest of the world by a red squirrel.

Nidhugg's only food is the roots of the World Tree—the roots that hold the whole universe together.

233

Name:	NIXIE
How to say it:	NIX eee
Where it lives:	Scotland
Where the myth or legend started:	Scottish legend

Legend

Nixie looks like a beautiful horse, but she has a large beak like an eagle. She is all black, with a beautiful flowing mane, and a white star on her forehead.

Nixie always lives near a river or stream, and tries to lure young girls close to the water. Sometimes Nixie visits a farm, where she makes real horses stampede. Then she leads them to the river, where they sometimes drown. Nixie also wanders near houses, offering rides to children.

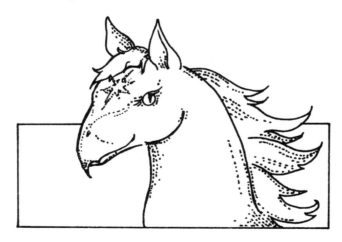

Not every Nixie is evil—there are friendly, helpful Nixies, too.

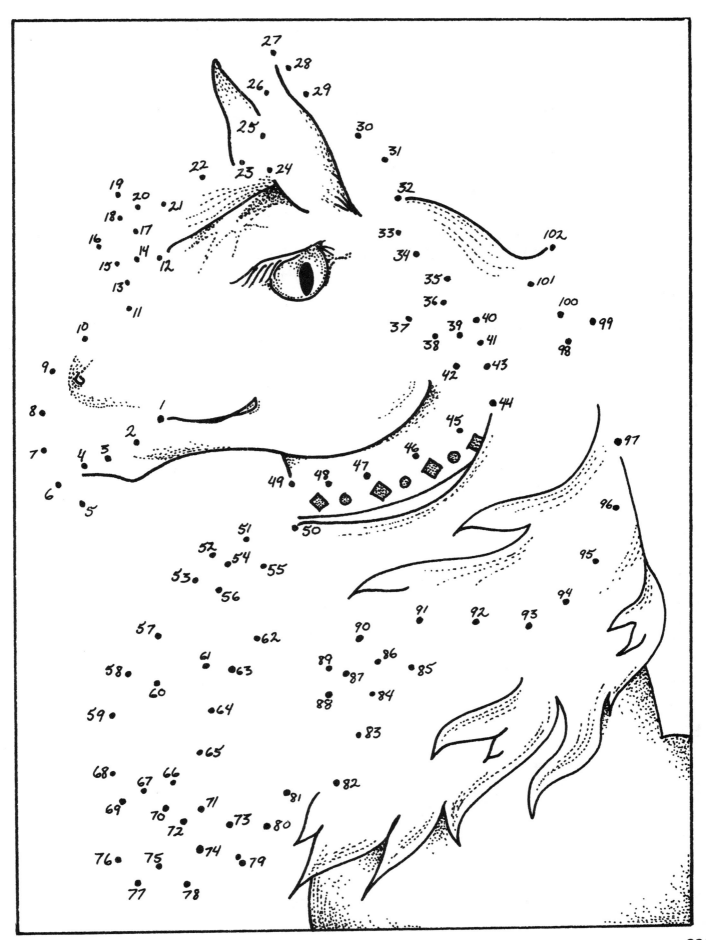

Name:	ORTHROS
How to say it:	OR throse
Where it lives:	On an island in the land of the setting sun
Where the myth or legend started:	Greek mythology

Legend

Orthros was a fierce guard dog with two heads. His job was to guard the cattle of another monster. The cattle were man-eaters, so *they* were dangerous too!

Orthros was such a fierce dog that Hercules was asked to kill it. Hercules did succeed in killing Orthros, and he captured the killer cattle, too.

Here's another dog monster that had *three* heads. Its name was Cerberus and it guarded the entrance to the underworld. Some said it had only one head; others said it had up to 50.

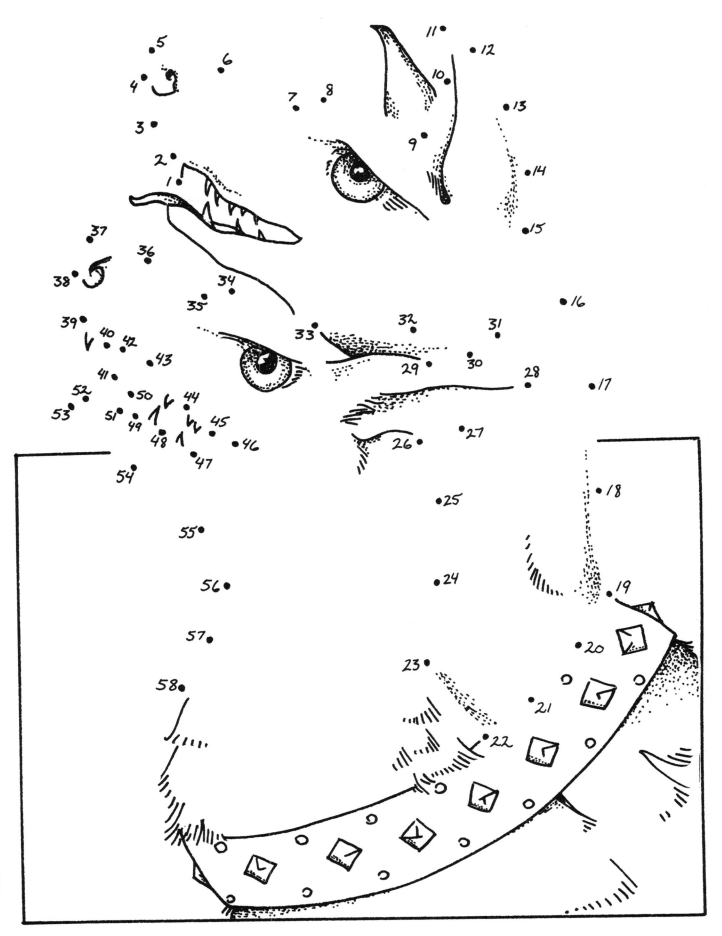

Name:	PEGASUS
How to say it:	PEG ah sus
Other name:	The Wind Horse, because he is as fast as the wind
Where it lives:	Corinth, Greece
Where the myth or legend started:	Greek mythology

Legend

Pegasus is a magnificent horse, created from sea, sand and the blood of Medusa, a snaky-haired monster.

Pegasus has beautiful wings, and he can fly anywhere. It was said that he could fly right up to the gates of Heaven.

Only the Greek goddess Athena could tame Pegasus, and she used a golden bridle and reins when she rode him.

Pegasus is snow-white and has huge wings.

Name:	PHOENIX
How to say it:	FEE nix
Where it lived:	In the Arabian wilderness
Coloring tip:	Some people say the Phoenix is red and gold. Others say it is red and purple.
Where the myth or legend started:	Greek version of Egyptian mythology

Legend

On its 500th birthday, this bird collects cinnamon branches and builds a fire for itself. The old Phoenix is destroyed in the fire, but a new one is born from the ashes. This new Phoenix lives for 500 years, then builds another fire. A new Phoenix always rises from the ashes!

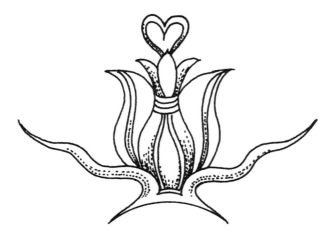

The Egyptian phoenix is a very beautiful bird, with a long crest. It sometimes wears a fancy headdress, or crown, something like this.

Name:	QUETZALCOATL
How to say it:	Indian way: kay tsal KO ahtel English way: ket ZAL ko AT el
Other name:	The Feathered Serpent
Where it lives:	Mexico and Central America
Where the myth or legend started:	Mexico and Central America

Legend

Quetzalcoatl was once a real person—a hero to the Indians of Mexico and Central America. He became honored as a wind god among the Aztecs and was an important ruling god to other tribes, too.

Over hundreds of years, people started to think of Quetzalcoatl as a huge snake with feathers. Carvings of the Feathered Serpent guarded their temples.

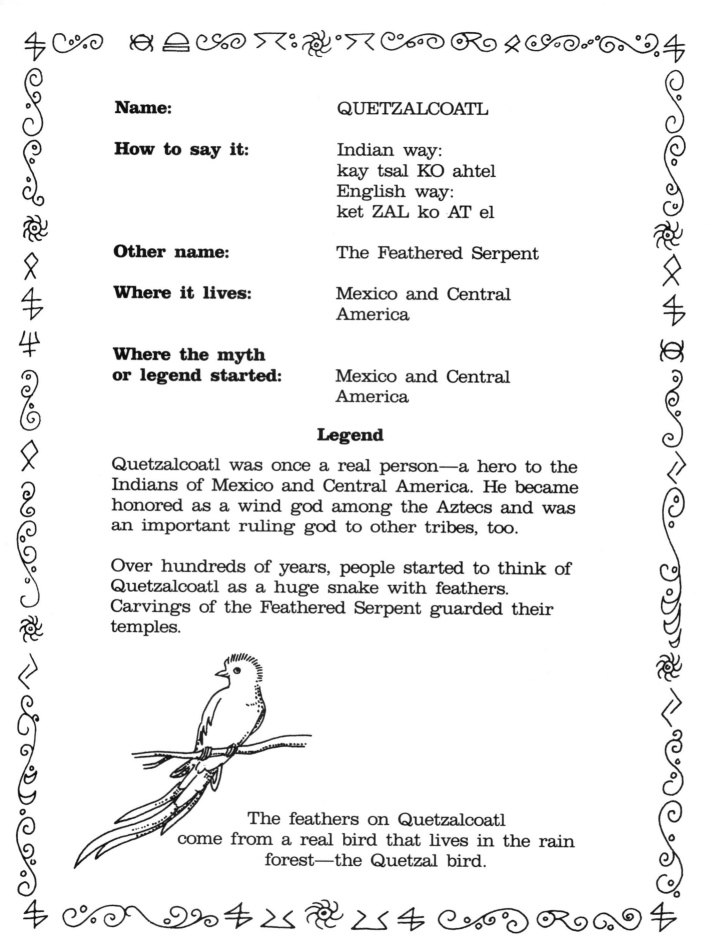

The feathers on Quetzalcoatl come from a real bird that lives in the rain forest—the Quetzal bird.

Name:	RAVEN SPIRIT
How to say it:	RAY ven
Where it lives:	Western North America
Where the myth or legend started:	Native American legends

Legend

To Native Americans in western North America, the Raven Spirit is a god with a sense of humor. This mischief-maker created mosquitoes just to bother humans!

The Raven Spirit isn't evil; it just likes to play tricks on people. The Raven also likes to hide things.

The story goes that if a real raven is killed, the Raven Spirit will make a lot of rain fall.

Raven designs are painted on clothing
and used on jewelry made by
Native Americans.

Name:	ROC
How to say it:	rok
Where it lives:	Arabia and Persia (the Mideast)
Where the myth or legend started:	Arabian mythology

Legend

Like the Phoenix on page 58, the Roc is a large, strong and beautiful bird. It has a crest with long feathers, and a large beak like an eagle.

The Roc is a rare bird; only a few people have ever seen it. It looks very mean, but it uses its magical powers to do good things.

The Roc has long, graceful head feathers.

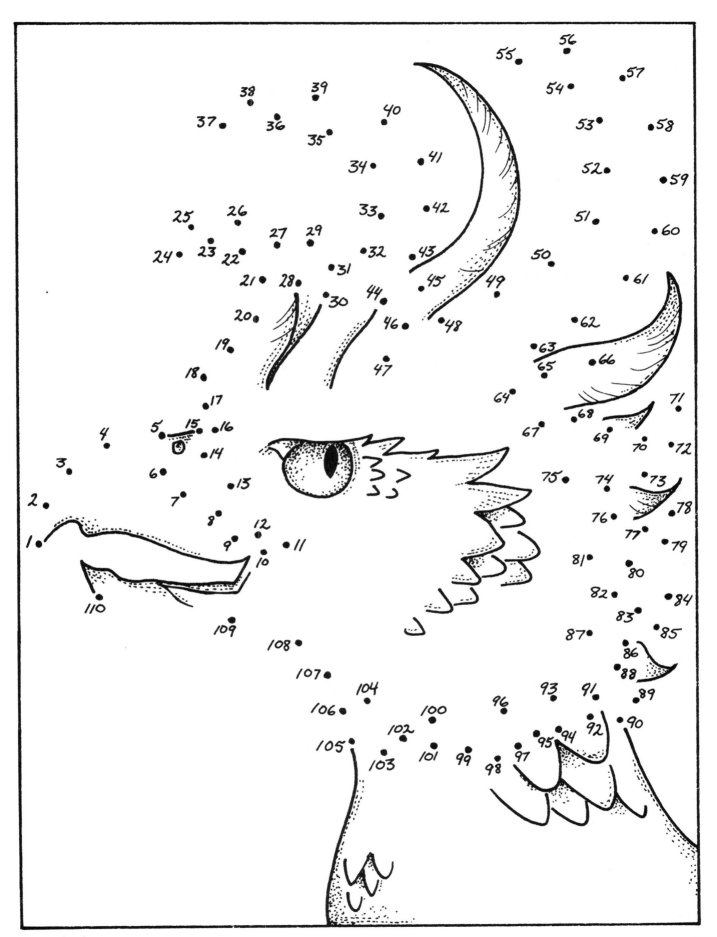

Name:	THOTH
How to say it:	Thoth (Like "both")
Other name:	Tehuti
Where it lives:	Egypt
Coloring tip:	Thoth wears a colorful headdress of blue, red and gold.
Where the myth or legend started:	Egyptian mythology

Legend

Thoth is the ancient Egyptian god of writing and learning. He is the inventor of letters, numbers and the calendar. Thoth also settled arguments.

Thousands of years ago, Egyptians made many carved and painted monuments to Thoth. They usually show him with the head of an ibis—a water bird with a long curved beak.

Thoth had great knowledge of magic.

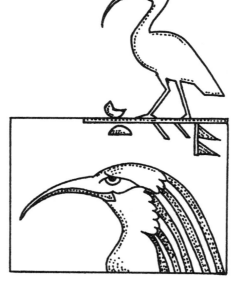

Name:	THUNDERBIRD
How to say it:	THUNN der bird
Where it lives:	North America
Where the myth or legend started:	Native American mythology

Legend

The story goes that thunder was created when a great eagle spirit, named Thunderbird, flapped its wings. Lightning was made by the flashing of the Thunderbird's eyes. Thunderbird was a guardian spirit that was very much admired. Even the feathers of an eagle were said to have magical powers.

The name "Thunderbird" was probably invented by white traders, to describe the bird spirit.

This is one of many kinds of Thunderbird designs.

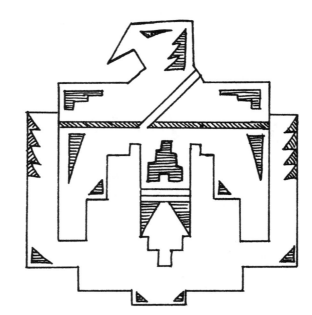

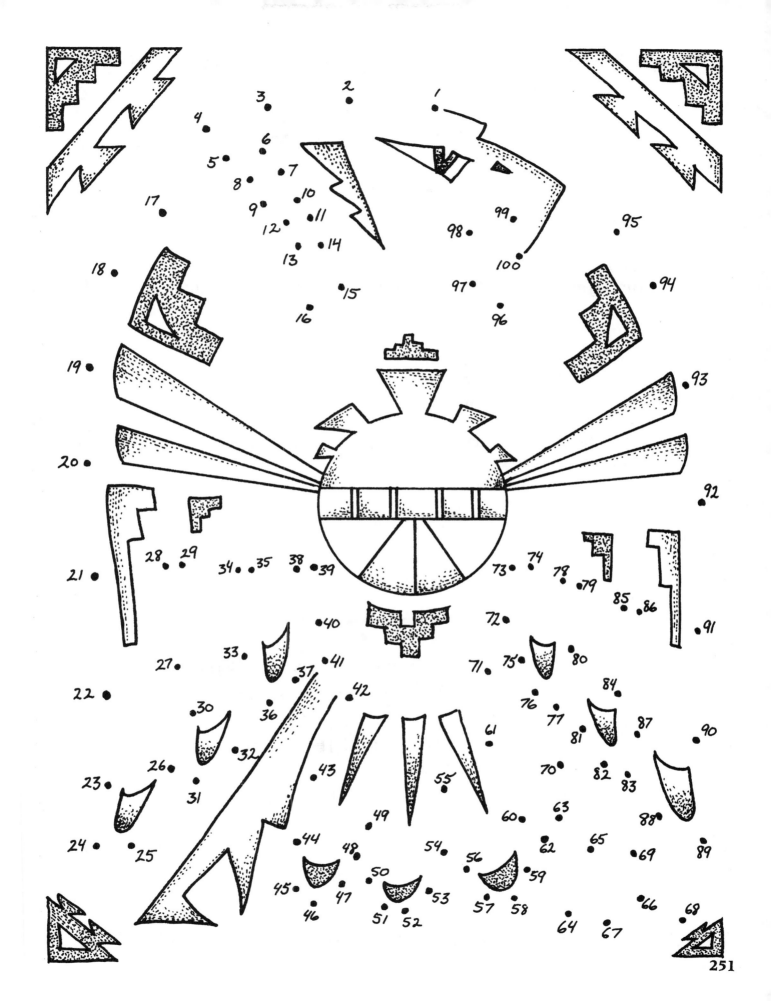

251

Name:	TIBETAN DRAGON
How to say it:	tih BET an
Where it lives:	The mountains of Tibet
Where the myth or legend started:	Tibet

Legend

Tibetan dragons have large eyes, and big teeth. They have the claws of an eagle, scales like a snake and the long flowing tail of a horse.

The story goes that these dragons like to follow the clouds across the sky.

Tibetan dragons live high in the mountains.

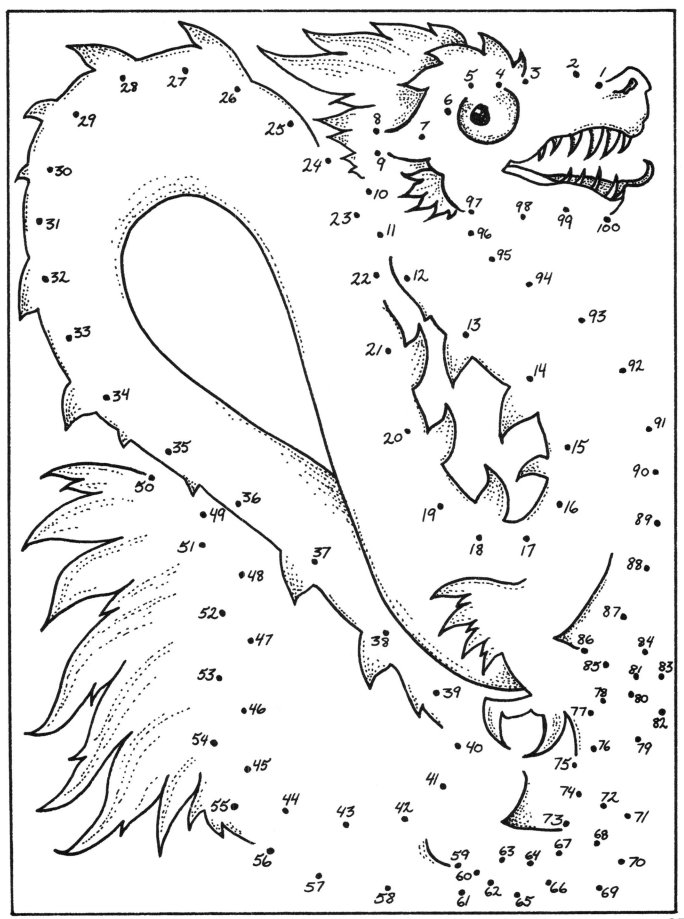

Name:	UNICORN
How to say it:	YU nih korn
Where it lives:	Europe, Great Britain, India
Coloring tip:	Unicorns are white, and they have beautiful blue eyes.
Where the myth or legend started:	Roman legends

Legend

The unicorn is a rare forest animal. One long horn grows from its forehead. Powder scraped from the horn will cure anyone from the most deadly poisons.

Unicorns are very hard to capture. Only a young girl can lure a unicorn from its hiding place deep in the forest. Some stories say that this animal has the body of a horse, while others say it looks more like a deer or goat.

Unicorns may be fierce; but some are so gentle, they could never harm another forest creature.

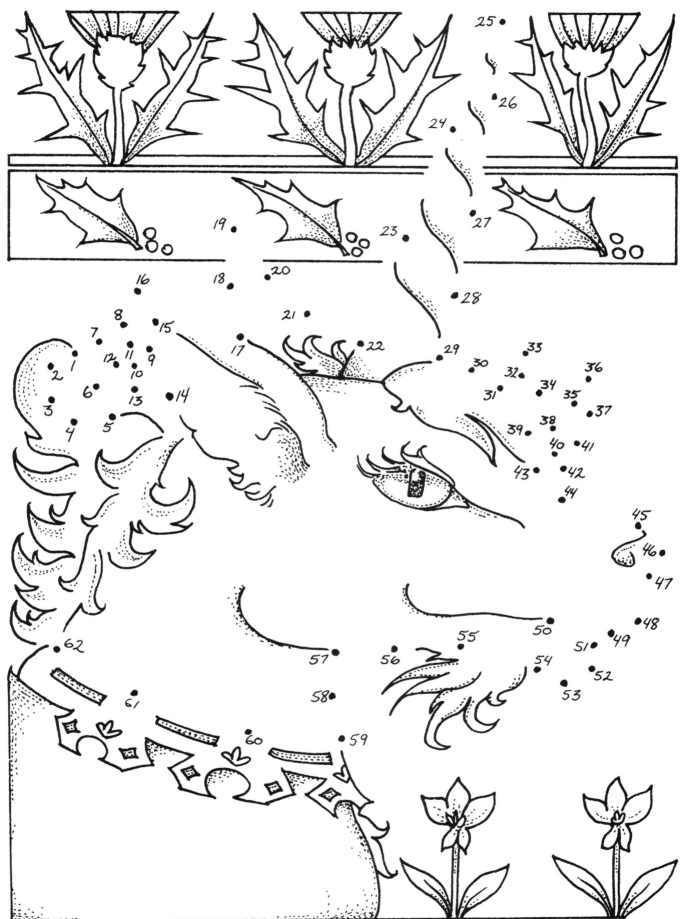